The Child's Own Story

Delivering Recovery

Series edited by Patrick Tomlinson, Director of Practice Development, SACCS

This is an essential series on practice for all professionals and parents involved in providing recovery for traumatized children and young people. Each book offers a practical and insightful introduction to an aspect of SACCS' unique and integrated approach to children traumatized by sexual, physical and emotional abuse.

of related interest

Therapeutic Approaches in Work with Traumatized Children and Young People
Theory and Practice
Patrick Tomlinson
ISBN 1 84310 187 4
Community, Culture and Change 14

Trauma, Attachment and Family Permanence
Fear Can Stop You Loving
Edited by Caroline Archer and Alan Burnell for Family Futures
ISBN 1 84310 021 5

Developing Adoption Support and Therapy
New Approaches for Practice
Angie Hart and Barry Luckock
ISBN 1 84310 146 7

Creative Therapies with Traumatized Children
Anne Bannister
ISBN 1 84310 155 6

Connecting with Kids through Stories
Using Narratives to Facilitate Attachment in Adopted Children
Denise B. Lacher and Todd Nichols
ISBN 1 84310 797 X

The Child's Own Story
Life Story Work
with Traumatized Children

Richard Rose and Terry Philpot

Foreword by Mary Walsh

Jessica Kingsley Publishers
London and Philadelphia

First published in 2005
by Jessica Kingsley Publishers
116 Pentonville Road
London N1 9JB, UK
and
400 Market Street, Suite 400
Philadelphia, PA 19106, USA

www.jkp.com

Copyright © SACCS 2005

Library of Congress Cataloging in Publication Data
A CIP catalog record for this book is available from the Library of Congress

British Library Cataloguing in Publication Data
A CIP catalogue record for this book is available from the British Library

ISBN-13: 978 1 84310 287 8
ISBN-10: 1 84310 287 0

Printed and Bound in Great Britain by
Athenaeum Press, Gateshead, Tyne and Wear

For my parents for providing me with a positive childhood these children were denied; for my wife Paula and our boys, Ben and Callum, and the unconditional love we share.

Richard Rose

To Eddie and Jill, with love.

Terry Philpot

Every person has a story; the secret is to find it.

Anon.

The Child is Father of the Man.

William Wordsworth

Contents

Foreword

At SACCS we believe that children traumatized because of abuse have suffered harm to their person, their body, their innocence, their childhood, their emotional health, their spiritual wellbeing, and the right to grow up in their own family. Most importantly they are children; normal children to whom abnormal things have happened, ordinary children who have had extraordinary experiences. Because the harm they have suffered is often so profound, affecting both their external and internal worlds, we have developed an approach that seeks to reach the very essence of these children and focuses on their recovery.

Since 1987 we have been developing services to meet the needs of this very vulnerable group of children, most of whom are emotionally fragmented. We recognize the need to help the whole child recover, both in residential care and in family placement. There are three integrated strands to this important work: therapeutic parenting, therapy and life story work. This book is concerned with life story work but makes reference to the other two aspects of our approach because of the integrated nature of the work, to which I have referred.

As readers of this book will discover, through intensive research into the child's past, life story work enables the child to understand what has happened, when and where they have lived, who has cared for them, and, most important, the decisions that have impacted on their lives.

Because most of the children who come to us have experienced many placement breakdowns their histories are virtually lost. Children need to understand their history if they are to move on in their lives, and if we do not collect this information there is every chance that it will be lost for ever.

The life story worker carefully picks up the scattered shards of a child's life, putting them together with great sensitivity. A long process begins to help children internalize understandings and to explore the meaning of their life and identity. Without the opportunity to integrate this work into the rest of the therapeutic task, the chances of children being able to make sense of what has happened to them and put the past into place are very slim.

Richard Rose and Terry Philpot have written a comprehensive description of the approach to life story developed within SACCS, which they set in the context of what we know about children's development, attachment, identity, the effects of abuse and other matters.

We believe that life story is an approach that deserves wider application, so that it can be practised by workers wherever they are employed, be that in local authorities, the private or the voluntary sector. This book will be a resource not just for social workers but for others, like foster carers and teachers, who have responsibility for children.

The journey to recovery is a long one and it belongs to the child. The child is at the centre of everything we do – a principle exemplified by life story work.

Mary Walsh
Founder and Chief Executive of SACCS

Preface

First, a word about SACCS (see also 'The Story of SACCS' on p.151), which has pioneered life story work as featured here. SACCS came into being in 1987 and since that time it has worked with hundreds of children offering therapy, residential care and an independent family placement fostering service. In 1997 SACCS appointed one of the authors of this book, Richard Rose, as life story worker. He looked at conventional life story work and found it inadequate for the work that SACCS wished to do with the children in its care. At the time of writing, SACCS is working with about 60 traumatized children, all of whom are engaged in life story work.

We are especially grateful to Mary Walsh, Andrew Constable and Patrick Tomlinson, respectively, chief executive and co-founder, managing director, and director of practice development, SACCS, for their continuing interest and helpful comments on the text. To Mary Walsh also for contributing the Foreword and 'The Story of SACCS'.

The book is also informed, most importantly of course, by the work which Richard Rose and his team at SACCS undertake daily. We are grateful to two of the young people, 'Ashleigh' and 'Tidus', whose stories are told here along with those of other children, but who also shared with Terry Philpot their experiences of life story work. We also acknowledge the SACCS life story work team at Shrewsbury, who met with Terry Philpot to talk about their work and explain aspects of 'wallpaper work'. Their work, as well as their comments and observations, also inform this book. They are Emma Blakemore, life story practitioner; Phil Lawrence, life story practitioner; Rachel Oliver, life story coordinator; and Helen Torrington, senior life story practitioner. We also acknowledge the work of the life story team at Tamworth: Sarah Goodman, life story co-ordinator; and Lynne Jones, senior life story practitioner. Carolyn Butler, a home manager with SACCS, introduced wallpaper work which has proved invaluable in life story work. We also acknowledge the work of the SACCS practice development team.

We are grateful to Ben and Callum Rose for the illustrations of 'Feelings' on page 95, 'Mum and Dad' (but not their own!) on page 125 and the 'Angry Cat' on page 127.

We have to thank Professor Martin Davies, late of the University of East Anglia and now with Norwich Primary Care Trust, who undertook some unasked-for research to explain to us the development of Maslow's hierarchy of needs (see Introduction).

The Social Care Institute for Excellence was kind enough to make rooms available for us when they met in London, and the staff of the Randolph Hotel looked after our needs when we met in Oxford.

It is important to point out that while the names of all children and adults in the case studies have been changed and some details have been altered to ensure anonymity, no details have been invented or embellished. The facts speak too much for themselves to be elaborated.

Writing this book has been very much a joint effort. We have spent many days together in discussion, questioning each other, exchanging ideas and opinions, swapping our own experiences of family life, as children and parents, and the complications and stories in our own families, while drawing out the details of life story work and the stories of children's lives and those close to them. During this process Terry Philpot wrote the text which we then both read together, commenting, changing, adding and excising.

The children whose experiences form much of this book are between four and 12 years of age and for that reason, and for ease of reading, we refer to them as 'children' rather than as 'children and young people'. For ease of reading, too, we have referred to children in the feminine and adults (whether staff, parents or others) in the masculine, unless, of course, we are referring to specific cases and situations.

Richard Rose and Terry Philpot

No Child is an Island

This book is an introduction to the process of life story work. It is intended for everyone who works with children and young people who have suffered trauma or who have been subject to multiple moves either through the lifestyles of the adults with whom they have lived or through the practices of the local authorities in whose care they have found themselves. These workers will be a very diverse group who will include adoption and fostering social workers; other social workers working with families and children (including those in child protection); child psychologists, psychotherapists and psychiatrists; long-term foster carers; members of youth offender teams; drug workers; members of child and adolescent mental health teams; and residential care workers. It is also intended for those who manage these services, as they can be instrumental in introducing innovative ideas in practice. We would recommend that those who work with young children on life story should be aware of child protection issues and ideally hold a qualification such as a BA in Social Work with experience of direct child and family social work.

The intention of the book is to enable workers to recognize and work with children who have suffered early trauma and may thus suffer problems of attachment. While much is known about these children, too often the aim seems to be to contain them physically rather than to help them recover. In seeking that recovery, through an exploration of their past, the hope is that children can be helped to avoid that 'whole life's mourning', which Moore (1985) saw as one result of abuse and which can sever the normal child–parent relationship. This is no easy thing to do, as this book will demonstrate. But the long-term benefits for the children and society are far greater and far more productive than attaching labels to them and letting them slide inexorably, as such children too easily can, into the criminal justice system or the adult mental health system, or, even worse, to have them die by their own hand when the burden of what they have suffered becomes too much to bear.

Another kind of life story work

Life story work is now a long-established social work method used in working with children and also in reminiscence work with older people with dementia.[1] It is most commonly used with children who are being placed for adoption to give them a factual narrative about their lives and the lives of those closest to them as they embark on a new life with their new families (Ryan and Walker 2003). Of course, many children who are successfully adopted and placed in foster homes often have had brutal experiences at the hands of their previous carers. However, there are some children who, in part because of how their experiences have affected them, may never be able to find a new family. We believe that a deep, richer and more detailed approach can be taken to life story work and that it can be used with children who are not permanently placed with a new family. But a definition of the more traditional kind of life story work serves our purposes well:

> It is generally accepted that life story books should answer the what, when and why questions about a child's life experiences. They should also be used as a means to allow the child, without undue pressure, to express feelings about these events. Life [story] work is a means of unravelling confusion and discarding some of the negative emotional baggage which the child has carried for so long. (Connor *et al.* 1985)

Life story work is a therapeutic tool that deals with the child's inner world and how that relates to the child's perception of external reality.

We are not claiming that the method described here is superior to other kinds of life story work with children, rather that it is different and intended for a very different purpose. Life story work, as conventionally practised, is right and effective for the purposes which it sets out to achieve. Ryan and Walker (2003) show what can be achieved and how to go about it.

The difference, as we see it, is that what we describe, while called life story work, is different because it works with children in the most extreme circumstances – and they require to be worked with differently. It is about involving them in moving to a new life (wherever that may be) – but can also be an essential part of the recovery process for all traumatized children. This method was devised by SACCS. The organization employs the UK's only group of professionally qualified social workers working solely in life story work.

In looking at life story work it is important to emphasize a point made by Vaughan (2003) who writes:

> We believe that we must think in terms of life story work and not story books. Life story books used to be seen as the way in which social workers could help children understand their past. Our current thinking is that they frequently omit too much of the child's life that is hugely significant. In our experience children, just as much as adults, need to develop coherent narratives and that while this can be a difficult and complex process it is an essential one. (p.160)

Vaughan refers to shortcomings in life story books, which we discuss later (see Chapter 6, where we also look at how these can and must be avoided). He says that books often 'simplify' and 'sanitize' children's pasts and offer an 'incoherent and inauthentic' picture. We do agree with him about how much that is significant to a child can be omitted; why this happens and how to see that it does not is something we will discuss. However, we would not minimize the importance of the book as Vaughan seems to do, rather we agree with Ryan and Walker (2003) when they write: 'It is the process rather than the product which will reveal the most benefits for the children and the people involved' (p.160) We refer frequently to life story *work*, a part of which, or the end product of which is the book. However, as we will show in Chapter 9, the creation of the book should not be the end of life story work.

Our life story work attaches importance to the past as does the more traditional life story work. However, one way in which the two methods differ is how we define the past and what we think constitutes the past – is the past about the relaying of facts and information alone or is it also about what the child believes the past to be, even though that may not be, in a strictly literal and factual sense, true? Life story work is about the people in the child's life, what happened to the child and the reasons why those things happened. It is not, and cannot be, a simple narrative or description. For example, recording that a child was moved from a foster care placement is less helpful than explaining why it happened, which means revealing to the child the real reasons, rather than those which may have been given at the time.

The ultimate benefits, as well as the initial anxieties, of the life story process, so critical to children's recovery, are illustrated by the words of two young people, both 17 years of age.

Ashleigh is a very vibrant, open young woman who lives in foster care and has been in the care of SACCS for four years. She was emotionally and physically abused, and although there was no proof of sexual abuse, it is likely that that happened too. She has had seven placements. She has gained nine GCSEs, is undertaking a course in performing arts at her local college of further education, a part of which has seen her visit New York with fellow students. She hopes to pursue her acting ambitions at university in London. She said:

> I didn't want to think about my past; I wanted to go forward, not back. I didn't like doing it, I didn't write anything; I let them get on with it.
>
> But the process was good because I found out things that I didn't know. I had lots of stuff going through my head and I never knew where it all went, where everything fitted in.

Before I did life story, I wouldn't be talking to you. It was hard but it was a good experience because now I know everything that's gone on and it's now all in the back of my head and I don't need to think about it any more.

I wasn't shy before but I didn't like talking to people. I would never have gone to New York. Stuff was going on in my head and I would never have pushed myself to study because of that.

I like acting because I think that I like showing off but I wouldn't have wanted to stand on stage before [life story work] because I would have thought people would have known what I was thinking and they'd judge me because of what was going on in my head. Now I can go forward and not dwell on the past.

If I hadn't had life story I would probably have stayed moody and I'd flip quite quickly. I learned to control my temper and to be calmer and that made me more committed to school where I've done well.

Tidus is an articulate but slightly hesitant young man. He, too, has had eight placements and now lives in foster care and has been with SACCS since 1998. He has a history of very severe sexual abuse. He gained ten GCSEs and is now studying for three AS Levels. He said:

When I was asked about life story, I was anxious; I didn't know what would come up but I wasn't afraid of it. I think my brother would be better if he had life story but he's afraid. It was good that there was therapy at the same time so that I could talk to the therapist about what had happened at life story.

I didn't realise what I had bottled up until I talked about it with Gail [Matthews, SACCS home manager] and what you need is a little push, like life story, to drag that up. It was the process that was important, not the book at the end.

It changed my perspectives. I was very loyal to my mum but in life story I found that I wasn't. I used to think that my dad was all bad and mum was good but now I think some good things about dad and some bad things about mum. You get a more overall picture of that and all kinds of things.

We venture to say, then, that this work is far more demanding and involving than traditional life story work, not merely because of the problems and experiences of the children involved, but because it goes much deeper into their past and stresses very explicitly the relationship of the past to the success of recovery and the kind of future which can be opened for the child. The work, which, from the preparatory stage to the final production of the book, can take up to 18 months or 36 sessions, also involves much travel, visiting, research and interviewing. The life story process is also about internalization (see Chapter 6), which is not the aim of other forms of life story work.

Nobody should try to ignore what has happened in the past before moving on. But for traumatized children it is simply impossible to ignore the past and move on: for the past must be something which is understood, analysed and accepted as a means to progressing. As we shall see, concentration on the past and all that that entails is not a discrete thing that can be wrapped up, put away and forgotten. It is something which is often present, that accompanies children into the future and only later, at some point along that road, when what has happened can be finally laid to rest, is a less troubled future possible.

Truth, myth and magical thinking

Life story work involves taking children along their journeys step by step, not passing over events, facts and beliefs or making the assumption that a child has understood or accepted when that may well not have been the case. At each step it is necessary to ensure that the child has, first of all, listened, and then that she has understood. Like all of us, children listen in very different ways, and there are methods, which we will describe, that allow us to know, through words and pictures, what has been heard and what has been understood. The core of this is that truth, which children may need very skilled help to accept, destroys magical thinking and the distortion that comes with it. Fahlberg (1994) says of magical thinking:

> For the preschool child it is their magical and egocentric thinking that most affects the reaction to parent loss. These children think

they caused the loss, that it came about because of their wishes, thoughts or behaviours. Their propensity for magical thinking is usually reinforced by a loss and is, therefore, likely to persist long beyond the age at which it commonly subsides.

Adults hold responsibility for trying to identify the specific magical thinking of the child they are working with or parenting. What does the child think he/she did that caused the move? Or what could the child have done to prevent it? What does he/she think could be done to have the desired outcome? These are questions the adult, not the child, must answer. (p.138)

Fahlberg goes on to say that magical thinking sometimes

takes place on an unconscious basis, particularly when it reflects the 'good vs bad' or the 'big vs little' struggles so commonly associated with this developmental stage [preschool years]. Behaviours may provide clues to the child's misperceptions. Carers, both before and after the move, should listen for comments that seem to make no sense, noting any odd or peculiar statements or behaviours. If carefully examined, these frequently give clues as to this child's perceptions and magical thinking. (p.138)

While Fahlberg is concerned with the moves of children through the care system, what she says is valid for those other events in children's lives which provoke magical thinking.

Magical thinking, then, is a way children fill in the gaps in their knowledge. When they don't know, they make it up. For example, a foster placement breaks down and the child is moved to a new home, but why did the breakdown happen? If the child blames herself for the breakdown (as she may well do), then she will conclude the same again when the next breakdown occurs (as well it might). It is safer for a child to believe this, but it only adds to her confusion about why she is where she is. The effect of this is taken through life – children who have filled the gaps in their own lives with their own fantasies, theories and stories do not become adults who are suddenly apprised of the truth.

Life story work helps to give meaning to magical thinking: it explains why children have believed what they have believed to be the truth about their lives, and helps them to understand distortion and deal with their lives. It allows them to confront their demons.

The children about whom we write here have been deprived of a normal family life and, with it, one of the functions of family, which, Fahlberg (1994) tells us:

> is to provide continuous contact with a small number of people over a lifetime. The long-term relationships between family members allow each person an opportunity to clarify past events and reinterpret past events in terms of the present. Children in care are frequently denied these opportunities. They change families; they change workers; they may lose contact with birth family members.

If a child has, say, ten placements (by no means unlikely), then she may have ten sets of foster brothers and sisters and ten sets of foster grandparents, with all of whom she may have to make or choose to make emotional investments. This becomes both emotionally exhausting and emotionally unproductive. It is far easier and safer for a child to resort to imagining what people think of her or imagining why she is in the situations that she is in.

We have referred to the differences in the two types of life story work. The conventional book seeks a clear, sequential and factual narrative. That can be adequate and useful, but for the kind of work described here, seeking a sequential narrative would be to impose something artificial. For these children often have a distorted view of their lives and one of the things which aggravates their situation is, for example, that they will test out their carers – and by so doing often destroy their relationships – in order to make sense of that distortion. The way to make sense of the distortion is for the child to come to understand, through life story work, that that is, indeed, just what it is – a distortion – and to learn how their view of their lives has become distorted. This work can, then, lead to a clearer vision.

While, at the end, there is, indeed, a book, its creation, what has gone into making it, is part of the healing, a part of the recovery. Death, grief, loss and separation are the common lot of traumatized children. The writing process helps them to explain that, and the final version can be a sign that the child has achieved an explanation and survived.

Trust and respect

Respect is key to the work: when the worker respects the child, the respect will be reciprocated. The word 'respect' requires a special mention. We could have referred to the child trusting the worker. But can the child trust, even if the worker believes and hopes that she can? The terrible experiences which these children will have undergone would make trust a tall order, and so it may be an exception rather than a rule. After all, these children will have trusted many adults in their lives and one kind of abuse which they will have suffered is the abuse of that trust and its destruction.

And so, while the worker may believe that there is trust, and certainly hopes that there is, he should set his sights at a more practical and achievable level. That is to offer the child consistency, honesty and respect. Trust may, after all, have come to mean, in the distorted world which the child sees, secrets, confidentiality and covering up. Respect, on the other hand, is not liable to distortion and means that what the worker does is in the child's best interests. Respect is about listening to the child (something that has now become axiomatic in child protection work), but also about the child listening to the worker.

The hierarchy of needs

Maslow (1954) formulated the 'hierarchy of needs', which can be helpful in understanding the kind of children featured here. Maslow's theory posits seven needs which all human beings ultimately seek to satisfy.[2] They are, in ascending order:

- Physiological needs – to satisfy hunger, thirst, sex and sleep
- Safety needs – to feel secure from physical danger
- Social needs – to belong, to affiliate with groups, to be loved

- Esteem needs – to be respected by others and to enjoy self-respect
- Cognitive needs – to have knowledge and understanding
- Aesthetic needs – the appreciation of beauty
- Self-actualization – the realization of one's full potential.

These needs have some resonance for social work, which, as Davies (2000) has pointed out, tends to be most concerned with the first four levels, exemplified, respectively, in the provision of material aid, child protection, referral to day care facilities, and counselling.

But if we look at traumatized children we can see a special relevance here of all levels of need. Children cannot move up the hierarchy, unless each level is satisfied. Thus we can say:

- At the first level at least one aspect of their physiological needs – which may often be sexual – will have been grossly distorted by their experiences.

- When it comes to the second level, they lack a sense of safety and, indeed, are in unsafe situations.

- The third level – social needs – has often been destroyed. Associating with others is made difficult by the betrayal of trust by those whom they felt they could trust, and they often feel unloved.

- The fourth level – esteem – has been severely damaged so that they lack self-respect and self-esteem and they do not feel respected by others.

- The fifth level – cognitive needs – lies at the very heart of life story work. Maslow refers to knowledge and understanding and traumatized children need to understand what has happened to them, but they also require self-knowledge.

- The sixth level – aesthetic needs – is reached when the child is sufficiently healed and is able to appreciate the good things of life – art, books and music.

- The final need, to realize one's full potential, is the possibility which results from therapy and life story work, so that these children can feel liberated enough to make their own choices and for their own creativity to have some chance of expression.

The child's world

No child is an island. In working with children on life story work we also have to work with those adults whom they have known – parents, brothers and sisters, aunts and uncles, grandparents, neighbours, the courts, the police, foster carers, teachers, nursing and medical staff, social workers: people who have tried to help them, people who have harmed them.

Techniques have to be learned to gather information from these people. Not least of the problems is how to find information when we are told that there is none. This may not only mean that information does not exist but also, for example, a local authority may say that there is no information to be had from an abusive father because he will not talk. An objective of this book is to show how we can go about the extensive information gathering that is required; how to communicate with the child; also how to overcome the obstacles which, wittingly or unwittingly, are put in our way.

In doing this we are learning how to create a life story book that incorporates the whole of the child's experience, which must include, in case we forget, celebrating the child's life. We made a point earlier of referring to the factual narrative of the traditional life story book. Our kind of life story book is not one which will excise all fantasy, all that is not factually true. Fantasy and fiction in relating our lives is not confined to traumatized children; it is an almost inevitable way in which most of us relate to others, one of our essential ways of dealing with the world. No one talks factually about their life; their story will be embellished with hopes, illusions, misconceptions and subjectivity. This does not mean that we lie, and it does not mean that what we say is harmful. Krog

(1998), in her book *Country of My Skull* about South Africa's Truth and Reconciliation Commission, refers to the tension in the commission between seeking truth and justice. She goes on to say something that is as relevant to life story work with traumatized children as it was for those, both perpetrators and victims, who appeared before the commission:

> If it [the commission] sees truth in the widest possible compilation of people's perceptions, stories, myths and experiences, it will have chosen to restore memory and foster a new humanity, and perhaps that is justice in its deepest sense. (p.16)

If we recognize that we explain our own lives to ourselves and to the world in the way described, then it is even more important that we recognize that traumatized children do the same; for them, perhaps more than for the rest of us, it can be a way of explaining an otherwise inexplicable life, of coming to terms with otherwise unendurable experiences, of facing otherwise unpalatable truths. Krog (1998) refers to the consequences for a community if it tries to wipe out a part of its past, which, equally, applies to individuals: 'it leaves a vacuum that will be filled by lies and contradictions, confusing accounts of what happened'.

Several things unite traumatized children. First, most of them have experienced a number of moves in their lives. Second, many of them suffer from an attachment disorder. This may not be in the clinical sense, but they exhibit many of the characteristics of the disorder and that is the label which has been given to them. Third, all of these children have a history of abuse – physical, emotional and sexual abuse or neglect, and often a combination of some or all of them. When they come to SACCS this may not be known or may be known imperfectly. It is working with them in a very intense way, a part of which is life story work, which unveils their truth.

CHAPTER 1

Who Am I? The Importance of Identity and Meaning

The meaning of meaning

For everyone, our understanding of who we are and of our place in the world – how we relate to those around us, as well as in the wider world – is critical to our emotional wellbeing. This sense of identity, this sense of self, shows in how we relate to others and how we present ourselves in our day-to-day relationships, from the most intimate to the most casual. It determines not only who we *think* we are but also who we *say* we are. In developing our sense of self we come to an understanding of who we are, what we are and why we are as we are. A sense of self is about individuality, our uniqueness as a person: I am who I am and no one else is like me. We attempt to find some kind of pattern or meaning in the experiences which have brought us to the point we have reached in our lives. We come to understand where we fit in, even if we are not comfortable with it. Acceptance of who we are is a sign of maturity.

Identity is a result of experiences that go to the very root of what it is to be human, a root perhaps too entangled in our being to be satisfactorily understood. However, Levy and Orlans (1998) state: 'Identity is whom the child believes him- or herself to be. Identity formation is based on the child's experiences, interpretation of those experiences, others' reactions to the child, and the significant role models the child identifies with'.

Children in care often have a negative sense of themselves, a damaged sense of identity. What they have known in care or within their families has negatively affected their sense of self; they have a poor view of themselves, they will often believe that the misfortunes which have come their way – from the abuse they have suffered to the breakdown of foster placements – is their fault. Children can come to see abuse and rejection as their lot in life, and this breeds a lack of trust in their relationships with adults. Indeed, they may actively sabotage relationships because, as they see it, they do not deserve them.

Thus, the sense of finding meaning, of understanding patterns and linkages, can be denied to a child who has been traumatized. Such children can, without help, grow into damaged adults, wreaking in the lives of others the same turmoil, harm and pain that they themselves have experienced. When the opportunity to engage in life story work is not available, and the individual has not been able to consider cause and effect, identity and a sense of self, it is possible that adults and children alike can become anxious and turn against themselves with drugs, alcohol, self-harm and, at the most extreme, suicide. One characteristic of such individuals is a lack self-esteem, the opposite of what has been referred to as 'personal judgement of worthiness...expressed in the attitude that the individual holds towards himself' (Coopersmith 1967). Of course, one does not have to have had an abusive childhood to have a low sense of self-esteem or to feel a lack of self-worth, but the child who has been abused and traumatized will have had all sense of worth taken from her and can experience this lack of self-regard *in extremis*.

A child can be so damaged that she cannot understand what for most of us is most fundamental. For example, a child may know who her mother is, but not understand why she cannot live with her. But, more fundamentally, the question the child will not be able to answer is what it means to be a mother (or a father). What does it mean even to *have* a mother and a father? Simply the presence of a mother and a father, but even when they are present what is their role vis-à-vis the child? How are they supposed to relate to the child? What do they do for and with the child?

Meaning entails having knowledge. Take the example of a child who has been taken into care. She has lived in a children's home and has also been in the care of one, two, three or even more foster carers. But can this child understand why she cannot live with her mother and father? To say that they could not look after the child is insufficient if the child is to understand who she is, why she has lived as she has (and with whom) and how this has led to her acting as she does. It would be very easy, in the distorted views that some children in these circumstances can develop, for a child to blame herself not only for who she is but also for her not being loved, even for the break-up of her parents' relationship. A child like this will need to understand that it is not her fault that such things happen, rather that certain events, not of her making, have affected her life. The child also needs to know that for all the awful things that have happened in her life, there have also been some good things – that there are people who have given love, people who tried to help, incidents that were enjoyable. This truer, more realistic, more balanced view is one which a child can then integrate into her understanding of her self and her identity and gives her a more rounded view of her life.

A part of that understanding is acceptance. There are two kinds of acceptance. One is to accept what has happened and to try to understand it as a basis for the future. The other is to know what happened, to believe that the past cannot be understood but that the present can be an opportunity to build a different future. This can be a denial that the past does affect us, and such an acceptance can bring later troubles. If children do not make sense of what has happened to them, then the past can catch up with them.

Race, culture and identity

The Children Act 1989 states that the child's ethnic, cultural and religious background should be respected and, where possible, cultural and religious needs should be met in any family placement. This is because our ethnic, cultural and religious background is something else which is critical to that healthy sense of self, of knowing who we are, what has made us, where we came from. Children who have suffered many placements, who have been separated from their families may well be unaware of their heritage or a part of their heritage. Even a child of, say, a white mother and a black father may not know her father's precise ethnic background if the father has been only a fleeting (or even a non-existent) presence in her life. There is plenty of evidence to show that the denial of a child's ethnic heritage can have a deleterious effect upon mental health[3] and that ignorance of it can, at the very least, be confusing to the child. So, helping the child connect to her religious, cultural and ethnic background is something which will also help to increase the sense of self, of who she is.

Those engaged in life story work will need to take account of the needs of children who come from black and ethnic minority families, or whose heritage is mixed. Such a background, as Ryan and Walker (2003) remark, 'is an added dimension to their feelings about themselves – colour'. They go on to say:

> Preparation for life story work always needs to be handled with extreme care and honesty, especially when you are trying to put things into their true perspective, and possibly even more so when you are working with black children and black children of mixed parentage – and particularly if you are white. (p.45)

It is necessary in life story work to enter into the child's world and understanding, which means that it is important to recognize the challenge that that presents with the child who is from an ethnic minority. This is especially so if the worker is white. Such a worker would be advised to make use of a consultant on race, but also to become familiar with the relevant aspects of the child's background – their religion, the customs and beliefs and practices in the country from which their parents come (or from which, of course, they may come).

As Ryan and Walker (2003) caution, black people are often thought of as a homogeneous group, something which no white person would ever consider true of themselves. Workers who take time to familiarize themselves with a child's background are saying something very positive to that child: that they respect and value her.

Race is often referred to but matters of culture and religion less so, though the three can be intermingled. Let us take four examples. The first case concerns a boy whose father was a Muslim from Bangladesh. The father would leave to go on pilgrimage, but so far as the boy was concerned, ignorant of his father's religion, he simply had a father who disappeared frequently – why he had no idea. The boy needed to know not only why his father left for such long periods but also the significance of why he did.

Another boy came from Tyneside, but he had no idea of his background or of the traditions of an area of which he had little memory, living as he was in the south of England. His mother, a Tynesider herself, had always been reluctant for him to know about his background because his father, who also came from the area, had gone to live in Wiltshire from the age of five to 15. The father had lost his Geordie accent, which had made him an object of ridicule among his contemporaries when he returned. Part of writing the boy's life story book was to hear a tape recording of his mother and a past foster carer so he could listen to their accents, and also to have copies of the local newspapers to read to acquaint himself with the area.

The third example concerns a girl who was of Irish descent, something of which she was unaware. Her life story worker took her to Ireland and she learned about Catholicism, the faith into which she had been baptized but had not been told about. She decided that she wanted to go to mass and to attend a Catholic school. When it was time for her first communion, her sister's first communion dress, thought to be lost, was acquired and she wore it at the mass. Again, this was an important connection with a hitherto unknown past. For another child in this situation, the matter might be dealt with differently but to the same end. Such a child, also baptized as a Catholic but brought up in ignorance of this, could be shown her baptismal certificate, told who her godparents are and the role of godparents, and taken to mass.

Last is a boy who had a white, Irish Catholic mother and a Muslim father. They were not married but the father was married to someone else and had four children. The son, though, had been brought up as a

Muslim (with his mother's agreement) and his father arranged that the local imam come to the house to teach the Koran, and so he remained ignorant of his mother's religion. The boy disliked the imam's visits and Islam gave him no reference points because his whole environment was non-Muslim. He did not attend mosque and was learning a language that he would not practise. However, had his mother not been antipathetic to her own faith, the boy could have made positive choices about which faith he wished to adopt. Here was a case where there was identity without meaning attached to it. The boy's situation was exacerbated by the local authority refusing to place him within any one of three white families, all of whom would have been suitable for long-term fostering solutions, while it sought a Muslim family. Failing to find one, the local authority then placed the boy with a Sikh family on the basis that Sikhs and Muslims are members of ethnic minorities!

Attachment

Important, too, in the formation of identity and a sense of self are the ideas of attachment, separation and loss.

Attachment theory was developed in the 1950s by John Bowlby (see Bowlby 1969).[4] It seeks to explain why patterns of behaviour either persist or change, over time and across relationships. It posits the idea of a blueprint that is created for each of us in the early months of life. This says that if our attachment stems from a nurturing and loving relationship, then we will develop maturely. But if the relationship is one of violence, rejection, pain, abuse, lack of bonding, and disruption, then there is a possibility of developmental problems, such as criminal, violent or abusive sexual behaviour.

In its earliest formulation attachment theory emphasized the parent–child relationship, and while that relationship remains formative, it is now also known that other relationships throughout our lives impact on our attachment. Children who have suffered long periods of separation from their parents or who have lost their parents and suffered severe emotional difficulties find it extremely difficult to make relationships with others and can become withdrawn. They can exhibit various other kinds of behaviour problems. While Bowlby and others based their ideas on close observation, the effects of loss and separation on children had been seen some while before this with the experience of children evacuated during the Second World War.[5] Howe (2000) says that 'attachment behaviour is an instinctive biological drive that propels infants into protective proximity with their main carers whenever they experience anxiety, fear or distress' (p.26).

Anxiety, loss and distress are, of course, an inescapable part of living but crucial to facing and dealing with them is whether one has sufficient emotional protection. Critical for the child is what is called 'the internal working model'. This is the mechanism through which the child attempts to connect her self, other people and the relationship between them. The quality of the child's caring experiences will determine whether the internal working model is positive or negative. According to Howe (2000), children's adaptation to their internal working model – their attachment style – can be

- securely attached (the carer is loving and the child is loved)

- ambivalent (the caregiver is inconsistent in how he responds and the child sees herself as dependent and poorly valued)

- avoidant (the caregiver is seen as consistently rejecting and the child is insecure but compulsively self-reliant) or

- disorganized (caregivers are seen as frightening or frightened and the child is helpless, or angry and controlling).

The last response is one often associated with children who have been maltreated. (It is important to stress that while we have referred here to children, a lack of attachment is seen in adults in their personal and sexual relationships and in their role as parents.)

Internal working models have also been referred to by Archer (2003) as 'road maps' providing the child with an internal framework of his world, which Perry (1999) calls 'experience-dependent'. This framework, according to Burnell and Archer (2003),

maps out the most suitable response-routes to familiar, and unfamiliar, challenges. IWMs [internal working models] reflect the child's view of, and confidence in, the attachment figures' capacity to provide a safe and caring environment. Moreover, these models, in turn, organise the child's thoughts, memories and feelings regarding attachment figures. Inevitably, they will also act as guides and predictors of future behaviour for the child and analogous attachment figures, such as adoptive parents. (p.65)

Schore (1994) refers to these models as being burned into the unconscious at the neurobiological level, and Solomon and George (1999) say that, once established, they are highly resistant to change as they assimilate change.

The essential thing about loss is that its effects can extend from the original object which is lost – say, the parent – to the foster carer, social worker, friends and family. Children can also become disengaged from school and the community. Those who experience a number of placements in care can undergo a double loss – that of a sense of belonging and of individuals and also of place as they may be situated hundreds of miles from their home, community and family.

Such explanations are, of course, psychoanalytical. However, we know that biological damage can result from abuse and violence which interferes with the growth of the brain, and that this damage manifests itself externally in various forms of disturbed behaviour (Perry 1999).

There is increasing recognition that even babies may suffer mental health problems as a result of early abuse.[6] As YoungMinds (2004) has explained:

The vulnerability of babies and toddlers to mental health problems is increasingly acknowledged. The effect of these problems on subsequent functioning – physical, cognitive and emotional – is being investigated widely. Research strongly suggests that the way in which the brain develops is linked to early infant relationships, most often with the primary carer. Whilst other relationships in later life can be crucial, for example relationships with adoptive parents, these primary infant/carer relationships have a key impact on the mentally healthy development of the child... Active, satisfying and reciprocal relationships with parents create the basis for a sense of inner confidence and effectiveness.

YoungMinds continues:

> There is evidence to suggest that the quality and content of the baby's relationship with his or her parents may effect the development of the neurobiological structure of the infant brain in a way that is harder to alter the longer the relationship patterns endure… Whilst we need to understand much more in this field, we are learning about serious, long-term consequences of neglect, trauma and abuse on early brain development and subsequent physical, emotional and social growth.

There was a time when biological and psychoanalytical explanations were regarded as inimical to one another. But it is no longer a matter of either/or but rather one of and/both if we are to understand the many ways in which human beings react to trauma as well as recover from it. Were the biological sciences as advanced 60 or more years ago as they are now, the neurobiologist and the psychoanalyst, each looking at the workings of the mind and seeking the reasons for human behaviour, might well have worked hand in hand. The forces of nurture and nature, we know now, are much more intertwined than was previously imagined.

Loss, love and hate

A simple approach to understanding children's emotional behaviour after loss, neglect and rejection is based on the work of Pat Curtis and Pat Owen (no date) and has been used as part of SACCS' life story training. Imagine two cups half filled with water. One cup represents a child and the other a primary carer and the water is the 'life essence'. The child is naturally inclined to relate and will, therefore, give some of their essence to the adult in the expectation that this will be reciprocated. Thus, the water levels remain constant and enriched. If the child does not receive from the primary carer, then her essence is decreased, and if she continues to give then soon little of her essence will be left. At some point, the child will realize that if she does not stop giving, she will run out of her essence and may, in a sense, die. To protect herself the child will cover the cup to prevent losing the last of herself. Unfortunately, with a cover on the cup she will not receive any essence and she remains in the chaotic state which caused her defensive action. Life story is a way in which children can gently learn to loosen the cover and begin to refill their cup with essence through exploration, knowledge and realization. This process is akin to Maslow's hierarchy of needs (see Introduction), as the child needs to move from her primary state to take safe risks and then, through trust and respect, to begin to gain esteem. However, children who have been traumatized can revert *down* the hierarchy or never move up it, seeking those points which are safe (like being fed and clothed) in the (mistaken) belief that they can then look after themselves because of the dangers of trusting in adults.

A child who has been abused can still feel a sense of loss of the person who was the abuser. Many abused children love parents who have abused them, and their separation from them when they go into care or the abusive parent is sent to prison is for them a significant loss. Such loss is sometimes not just emotional but has other consequences (see the case example 'Kylie: A child alone').

Kylie: A child alone

Kylie was two when her father went to prison for 18 months for fraud. Her mother was an alcoholic and was 20 years younger than her husband, who was a father figure to her. When he was imprisoned she was unable to care for herself, let alone her child, and Kylie put herself to bed and fed herself. Her father later returned to his family but he, too, began drinking heavily, and Kylie was caring for herself almost entirely until she was taken into care at the age of six. Her mother died when she was ten. At 14 she remained in contact with her father, now aged 66, but she said: 'When my father went into prison that was the start of all my troubles.'

Abused children do not want to lose their parents. Children who disclose abuse rarely understand that their parents could be punished as a result, and rarely want this outcome. Where the parent is removed or, in many cases, where the child is removed, the child begins to regret disclosure. If the child is abused subsequently, she may keep the secret to herself for fear that this will occasion more loss. What these children want is for the parents to stop abusing them. They may experience very complicated emotions – sometimes love and hate co-exist when directed towards those who have abused them. Life story work may cause this to change, and children's emotions and moods may swing. These complications may arise, in part, from their own sense of guilt: was it something they did which caused the abuse?

We can see from the above that the formation of a sense of self, of identity is a complicated and delicate process. A positive part of that, especially for those who have survived traumatic experience, is an acceptance of who they are and that they have emerged, come what may, into a state of recovery. In life story work, it is important to allow a child's history to be written and for her to express her values, and for us not to impose our own. In the words of a 17-year-old girl who was asked why it was she wanted to show her life story book to her boyfriend's parents, when it might affect how they viewed her: 'I am proud of who I am.'

Exercises

1. Think of your own childhood and consider your attachment figures and how they may have influenced you.

2. If you are a parent do you unconditionally love your children? If not a parent, do you believe that unconditional love is a prerequisite for a human being to develop healthily?

3. As the child receives unconditional love from her parents, does it naturally follow that that is reciprocated?

4. Do you believe that there is a conflict between the psycho-social model and the bio-neurological model which explains child trauma?

CHAPTER 2

A Tale of Two Children

Every child is an individual, every child is different; but children who have been abused, like children who have been loved and cared for, have certain things in common. There are patterns that life story work can reveal about their histories and those of their families. This is not to paint a deterministic picture, because being individuals, human beings buck trends, but understanding this can be helpful to those who work with traumatized children.

And so, who are the children about whom this book is concerned? Their stories or parts of the stories are told in the following pages. Anecdotes, incidents in their lives and those of their families, case examples, their own words – all these create a picture, or at least give some impression of a particular child, but considered together also allow us to draw conclusions about what happened to them and why. Knowing this is the key to their recovery.

But while such stories and other aspects of children's lives are given later, this chapter offers detailed histories of two children, whom we will call Penny and Anne. The detail of their stories illustrates most fully the problems which beset these children and many others like them – among them the extraordinarily fragmented families; the coming and going of different (often abusive) people in their lives; the lack of stability; and the sometimes unhelpful actions (or lack of action) by social services departments. The stories also show the magnitude of the task for those who help them along the road to their recovery.

Penny

As with so many children who feature in this book, the shadows that were to be cast across Penny's life could be seen before she was even born. In 1977 Georgie, her father, was convicted of removing a child from local authority care. He was then reported as living in a county in the English midlands with a young girl whom, it was said, he 'fostered'.

Penny has two brothers and two sisters older than her. One of them, Paul, is the son of Stan Preece, a man whom Penny's mother, Linda, was married to before she married Georgie. Her other older brother, Jake, is believed to be the son of Georgie's brother. One of the sisters, Julie, is the child of Georgie and Linda. These three children were freed for adoption but never placed, and were in local authority care. However, Penny knew little of this, and, indeed, had little knowledge of these children. Paul and Julie were involved in an incestuous relationship when in care, something else that Penny knew nothing about. Penny's second older sister, Clare, her senior by only a year, lived with Penny and her parents. Clare is also the child of Georgie and Linda.

The result of all of this was effectively to create for Penny two sets of brothers and sisters, neither set of which knew much about the other. While Penny's parents may have referred to the three older children, they were only shadows in her life. This was exacerbated by the social services department's refusal to allow information and photographs about them to be shared with Penny during life story work – and yet at this same time her brothers and sister were all in the same local authority's care and none of them were adopted or in the process of being adopted.

Penny's sister Clare was poorly cared for, but support was provided to Georgie and Linda, the children's mother, who seemed to respond to the advice. But when Linda was expecting Penny, Clare was rapidly losing weight. Social workers monitored the situation but took no action. In August 1989, less than four months before Penny was born, the local GP was concerned for the wellbeing of Clare as her parents had missed several appointments. Linda was also missing many of her antenatal appointments and this remained the case until she was rushed into hospital for an emergency caesarean two weeks before Christmas.

The bruises that appeared on Clare could not be explained, her home was unkempt, the family did not eat healthily, and there was concern about the way the parents cared for themselves and their children.

It took only three days after Penny was born for the GP to demand that a case conference be held to discuss Linda's 'limited capabilities'. However, the social services department disagreed with the heightened concern and decided that it was more appropriate for the health visitor to keep a watchful eye. While neighbours and health service workers raised more and more concerns, there was still no intervention by social services.

By February 1990, when Penny was two months old, an environmental health inspector for the council reported concerns for the safety of the children: the house was unfit for habitation, and council workmen said that they were not prepared to enter the building. There was no heating and there was damp and dog faeces.

But when a social worker visited she reported that the house was warm, although the family was living in one room. The GP was concerned that Penny had missed her post-natal checkups; when she was brought in she was dirty and poorly cared for, she had thrush and poor social development. By the turn of the year Penny and Clare had few toys and books and the house was in very poor condition.

Despite continuing concern, there was no case conference on either child and the social services department was not providing direct support or monitoring. However, a health visitor's report at the time said:

> The house was dark and cold; both girls were in the corner of the room. Clare was playing with a plastic bag and Penny was knocking her head against a wall. Penny hid her face and did not speak. All her visible skin and clothes were very dirty. Her hair was matted, and she had shadows under her eyes. Georgie called her but

she did not respond. Georgie sat smoking, flicking ash into an over-flowing bag of rubbish.

The health visitor requested a planning meeting and tried unsuccessfully to arrange a joint visit to the home with a social worker.

At six, Penny was attending Midway County Primary School. The children were unkempt and Penny was reported as soiling at school. It was at this time that the first concerns of sexual abuse were raised. This involved Tom Clunes – a powerful family member and Linda's father – and a young adult called Grace, a relative, who may have been his stepchild. No action was taken in the criminal courts but a civil court granted a prohibited steps order.

The family were successfully resisting social services' attempts to offer support despite more concerns being expressed by the head teacher of Penny's school. Yet again neighbours were telling the social services department that Georgie was hurting his children, who were heard screaming at night. A neighbour complained to the RSPCA about the condition in which the family's dogs were kept. The dogs were taken away.

In June 1996 the social services finally became involved with the family, when Derek Parker, a cousin of Georgie's and a Schedule 1 offender, lodged with the family.

That November, as Penny approached her seventh birthday and was attending school in nappies, the family were 'warned' that any more referrals would result in a case conference. They disappeared from the local authority area and were later found living in a neighbouring area. While there Clare alleged sexual abuse by Michael Trevelyan, a relative of David Trevelyan, a man with whom Linda had embarked on a relationship when her marriage to Georgie was breaking down, as it did periodically.

In January 1997, for reasons still unknown, the first authority closed the case. That year Linda and Georgie separated again and she moved, with Clare, Penny and Mark, her newest child, to live with her father, Tom Clunes, back to the area of the first authority. Concerns about neglect continued to be expressed by social workers and teachers in the authority from which she had moved, but nothing happened. Linda then moved to live with David Trevelyan, whom she was later to leave again, but with whom she had two other children, Shaun and Jodie. In June Linda changed all the names of the children to Trevelyan and did not tell social workers where she had gone.

David Trevelyan was now beginning to write to Clare, telling her that she was sexy, while Tom Clunes reported him as a sexual risk to the children and claimed that he was physically violent towards them. David then made allegations that the children told him that they were watching 'rudey videos' with their parents when the family lived together.

Despite these concerns the second local authority closed the case. Within a month referrals again were made about the children's safety and wellbeing. Clare, ten, Penny, eight, and Mark, six, were all still in nappies. Penny's nappy was stuck down with industrial tape and all the children had scabies. By July they still had scabies but had also developed eczema and impetigo and were suffering severe emotional and physical neglect. Linda had returned to live with David. The social services department reopened the case, there was a case conference but it was decided not to place the children on the child protection register.

When neighbours threatened to burn the family home down Linda moved away to stay with Tom Clunes, but for some months, until September 1998, the first social services department supported the family and attempted to help Linda improve her parenting skills. But there was little improvement and Penny was seen in school dirty and smelling of urine.

The social services department decided against legal action despite the fact that Linda was not co-operating. It also lost the family's records, which made court action even more difficult. Georgie then alleged that Tom Clunes, his father-in-law, had sexually abused Clare and a child outside the family. Linda and David's relationship was volatile and created an unstable environment for the children and they again separated.

In February 1999 Linda revealed to a social worker that a friend of Georgie had sexually abused Penny, but there was no record to confirm this. In April Penny and Clare said that their stepfather David Trevelyan and Ronnie Chucks, a friend of Georgie, their father, had sexually abused them. Penny withdrew her complaint when videoed, although Clare stated that David Trevelyan had touched Penny on her private parts.

Georgie returned to the family home in June and immediately Penny was seen to deteriorate, her incontinence became worse, she was very withdrawn, lacked friends at school, where she bullied, and was uninvolved. A record exists that Derek Parker, Georgie's cousin, the Schedule 1 offender, was still visiting the family home and that Penny had alleged he had sexually abused her. Later Penny, aged 10, was seen kissing Michael Trevelyan, aged 17. He had been previously warned for a Schedule 1 offence. In December Penny was found to be living with her grandfather, Tom Clunes.

Linda moved to a caravan site. It was later discovered that all the adults who had been the cause of concern in Penny's life had visited or were living on the site.

In mid-January 2000 Penny, Clare, Mark, Shaun and Jodie were removed from Linda's care and placed in foster care. Medical examination revealed clear evidence that Penny had suffered repeated vaginal abuse and possible anal damage. When in care all the children disclosed sexual abuse by David Trevelyan, and Penny also indicated that she was also abused by a man called Graham Larkins, a friend of David Trevelyan.

All the children alleged abuse by several adults: when asked what had happened, Penny referred to her abuse as being 'like always', by which she implied that abuse was customary. The Crown Prosecution Service felt unable to bring charges, although it concluded that the children were being truthful.

Penny was placed with SACCS prior to the final hearing, which agreed a care order. Contact with her parents was denied under section 34 of the Children Act 1989 within three months of Penny's placement.

Penny still struggles with her sense of self; she has a clear understanding of the facts of her past but has not been able to attach meaning to them. Forced to abuse her younger brothers and sisters, she is unable to accept that she is not guilty of this. Her questions centre on her misperceptions and the confusion she feels between guilt and loss. She has no family contact and feels separated from her reality. This itself caused negative feelings about herself and her self-worth, which inhhibited her recovery.

Where Penny has developed any understanding and identity it is through life story work, therapy and the work of those that care for her. She has much more to achieve, but her future looks positive and her placement should lead to her recovery.

Anne

Like Penny, what was to happen to Anne was prefigured by the experience of a sibling, in Anne's case a half-sister, Jackie. Social services first became involved with Mary Jones (as Jackie's mother then was) when Jackie was found abandoned in a park, with her father, Derek Jones, later found in a comatose state nearby. The child was placed for adoption soon after.

Mary Jones was born in 1961 and married Derek Jones in 1984 soon after Jackie's birth. She seems to have had good mainstream schooling followed by several jobs and work scheme placements. The Joneses were divorced in 1988. Mary Jones then met and, in 1993, went on to marry Harry Perkins, whom she met at a local day centre for people with mental health problems. Mary Perkins (as she became) was described as being poorly organized and prone to bouts of depression.

Her second husband was born in 1967 into a travelling family that settled in the north east of England. He was one of 16 brothers and sisters. Harry Perkins attended a special school for children with learning disabilities and never held a proper job. He suffers from epilepsy. Diagnosed as having paranoid schizrenia, he was detained under the Mental Health Act. He also had a learning disability, and it was felt that he would never be able to live independently. Mary Perkins also had a mild learning disability, as well as mental health problems.

Anne was born to the Perkins in November 1993. She was a healthy baby who weighed 7lb 10oz and there were no medical concerns. The Perkins were relocated to a council house in a particularly dilapidated estate, and due to the behaviour of both adults, the couple were targeted by locals and lived fearfully behind boarded windows.

During her pregnancy with Anne, the couple were unsupported by their families, and social services' involvement seemed limited to offering adult services. Harry would often bring people back to their house, and concern for the safety of Anne was expressed on numerous occasions.

As well as this concern was the doubt about the capacity of both parents to care for a child. The midwife expressed her concerns to the social services department and a consequent child protection conference agreed that Anne should be placed on the child protection register under 'neglect' before she was born and that both parents should be assessed for parenting training.

One month before birth, the family were moved to another house, this one again of poor quality. Neighbours immediately targeted the family.

As soon as Anne was born, there had been an application for a care order and social services was granted an interim care order. Anne joined her parents at a residential assessment centre, and the family stayed there for two months. The assessment went well and the local housing authority allocated them a hostel place. The interim care order continued till August 1994 when a supervision order was granted. As a result of the support to baby and parents, the Perkins had demonstrated their ability to care for each other and Anne, and so an assessment worker visited every two weeks.

This situation did not last long: within two months Anne was placed with her aunt and, following an assessment, moved to a foster care placement for two weeks. Over the following 14 months, Anne was placed with different foster families, and each time she was returned to her mother, although she was referred by various professionals for being physically and emotionally neglected.

By March 1997 it was obvious that attempts at rehabilitating Anne with her parents were failing. On the last occasion she had returned to her foster home with swelling to her vagina and showed some sexualized behaviour. Care proceedings followed, but the family insisted on taking Anne home and social services agreed.

Anne went back into foster care in April 1997, and in September her brother Raymond was born. Medical staff expressed concerns about Mary's attitude to Raymond and her family. He went into voluntary care three days later and Mary was referred to the mental health team.

Concerns were raised when Anne was in the care of a foster carer, Dot Robson. These were about how she dealt with Anne's screaming. The child would be locked in a conservatory or sent to her bedroom, which she was not then permitted to leave, and was left to cry. Anne was also dressed as a doll, and Dot was said to be 'obsessed' with cleanliness.

Anne was placed with new carers, and within four weeks was beginning to disclose sexual events involving family friends of her parents. Soon after, Raymond came to live with his sister and her carers. During contact Mary assaulted a social work assistant and abducted Anne and took Raymond, who, being accommodated, was not on a care order, with her. Two days later a family member tipped off social services about where Mary had taken her children. In a very public incident, police surrounded the family in the street with police dogs, removed both children and returned them to their foster home. In January 1998 an interim care order was granted to the social services department and contact was restricted to three times a week with two social workers to be present.

That same year Anne's other brother, Danny, was born. He, like Raymond, was to be adopted.

When Anne had contact with Mary both social workers and carers expressed their concerns. There was also concern at the fact that Mary was pregnant again. By April, Anne was refusing to go to meet her mother and was becoming very 'clingy' with the foster carer, who was also concerned about the heightened sexuality demonstrated by Anne towards her children and her husband.

In 1999, when she was six, Anne was placed with another foster family, while a freeing order for eventual adoption had been granted. Within four months the placement broke down.

At the beginning of January 2000 Anne said that she wanted to be dead, to have real wings and to fly away. She asked and pleaded for her new foster carer to kick her, to hit her and to throw her down the stairs. She was, at this point, wetting herself and behaving unpredictably. This behaviour increased, and by the middle of the month she was harming herself and damaging property.

In March the following year, after more respite care and rejecting those caring for her, Anne was referred to an independent fostering care agency, and in late May was placed with foster carers. By August she was violent, talking of death and showing 'obsessive' behaviour, although the obsessive part was not recorded in detail in her social services files. Her carers, like so many before, gave 28 days' notice of the placement to be ended. Anne was placed with SACCS in January 2002.

Anne has had 25 placements, some with the same carers, but these do not include the amount of respite foster care she has had, although it is known that the last eight carers required weekend support in caring for her. Her schooling suffered when she attended six different schools, four of these because of moves out of the local authority area. Her school behaviour caused concern, mainly in her inability to make friends, her violence towards other children, and her coarse language to children and staff.

Harry Perkins is in a secure hospital, while Mary Perkins lives, with support, in the community.

Anne was sexually abused while in her parents' care, very probably by people whom her mother and father knew, but nothing has ever been proven. She is now working towards her understanding of herself. She has been able to think and consider her past experiences and give some meaning to them. She still struggles with her feelings and emotions and often relies on her past behaviour, where she feels more secure despite this being 'wrong' for her.

Anne is a well-loved child but is unable to accept praise, because she cannot believe that she is good at anything and thinks that she is bad. However, her sense of self has been increased, which affects positively who she is and what she represents. She has established a foundation, which itself will lead to continued self-awareness.

CHAPTER 3

The Truth and Something Other Than the Truth

A lack of information?

Too often it is said about a child that nothing is known about this or that aspect of her past. This chapter starts not so much with the assumption that this is rarely true but in the knowledge that it is not. Life story work with traumatized children has demonstrated that there are always avenues to explore, sources to tap, people to talk to, documents to find, and information to be gleaned in constructing a child's past. The worker needs to know as much as he can and, in seeking that, to remember that few things are impossible or impractical.

First, we have to ask ourselves: what is it we are doing? The answer is that we are unveiling the story of a child, of her family and of others who have had contact with her, perhaps fleetingly, perhaps profoundly, perhaps helpfully, perhaps harmfully. Every effort must be made to talk to all of these people and to get their stories and elaborate upon them, that is to fill in blanks where their story is incomplete. Where these people cannot be reached, then we must endeavour to discover any form of documentation that relates to the child's life.

The most basic documents that relate to a child are the case files; yet, while they are the most readily available documents for social workers, they are frequently not consulted to reveal critical information about a child's life. It is almost as if the belief is that a past file can tell nothing about the present and so there is no need to read it. But past social work case files can reveal some of the most important aspects of life story – read carefully they can reveal patterns and processes that can throw a revealing light on the child's past and how she has come to be where she is and who she is. Indeed, many social workers, if they were to read all the files held on the child and her family, would make better decisions and avoid many placements, because they would be doing what is so important – learning from the past.

However, children are often moved from placement to placement without information – as they go into residential care, into foster homes, into school. They are in circumstances where they have been fed, clothed and sent to school – there is never (it is said) time to do anything else, because that is 'someone else's' job and part of that 'someone else's' job is to ensure that information about them is correct and up to date. Their records may not give their medical history; they may say where their parents live but not necessarily their address; or not say why the child is in care.

This is not helped by the number of placements that children in care can undergo. One child who went through the life story process was eight years of age and underwent 57 moves. In SACCS, where the average age of children is ten and the average number of moves is nine, many of the children have also lived with their mothers in women's refuges or with mothers' various partners at different addresses (see, for example, the case of Penny in Chapter 2), which in themselves do not count as placements. While the government has set a target that no child in care should experience more than three moves, even that is a large number for any child, let alone one whose life has been one of turmoil, change and confusion.

But no one's life is a mere collection of facts, any more than a person's body is a mere collection of molecules. Thus, in creating a life story book we are gathering everything that makes a human life – the facts, stories, anecdotes, memories, fiction, religious and cultural life, fantasy, expectation, loss and fulfilment, hope realized and hope dashed, family idiosyncrasies, the good and the bad. And we are not only seeking the testimony of other people because they have passed through the child's life and can tell us about the child: many children, for example, will have been in foster care and we need to remember that the lives and stories of those foster families are also those of the child. What do they believe in? What do they value? What are their stories? We have to ask this, because the children they will have cared for may have assimilated themselves into that family's world, often as a defence against their own world. In residential care, as in foster care, a child may adopt role models, may pattern herself on certain individuals or mirror someone to whom she reacts. If we are to understand and help the child understand why she is as she is, these are the very people to meet and to know.

Let us look at some of the factual and other information needed in life story work and how it can be obtained.

We need to consider practical planning. We need to be realistic and realize that while the search will be longer, deeper and more detailed than conventional life story work, there will be some information beyond our reach. For example, some people in the child's life will no longer be alive or may have gone abroad and not be traceable or not within a reasonable distance for visiting. Travel across continents would only be justified when no other source of information is available for that period of a child's life. However, the Salvation Army offers a free tracing service, as does International Social Services for people who have some overseas connection. But being practical should also mean doing what we *can* do. For example, a life story worker took a child to Carlisle where she had at one time lived but of which she had no memory. Walking the streets, looking at local shops, visiting the house where the child had lived and the house where the child's grandfather had lived served to prompt the child's memory.

Perhaps readers can best envisage the task of mapping a child's relationships by thinking what they would need to know about constructing their own life stories at the age at which they are now; who they would need to help in that; how they would find them; what other kinds of information would be required and how it would be obtained. The host of people would probably include parents, grandparents, brothers and sisters and other close relatives, teachers and head teachers, nursery teachers, clubs and associations of which the worker has been a member, and work colleagues. In the case of a child in care some of these would be relevant but, in addition, there would be child protection officers, other social workers, reviewing officers, foster family members, residential care workers, the police, among others (see Figure 3.1). We should not treat children as different from ourselves because all of us have people and institutions that have impacted on our lives and documents that can illuminate our past.

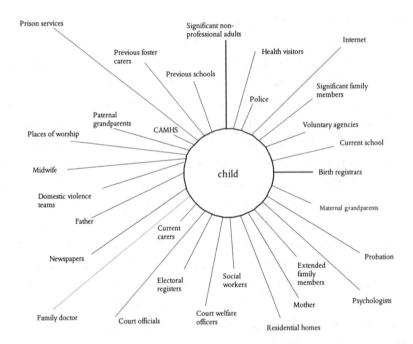

Figure 3.1 Sources of information to help construct a child's life story

Avenues to follow

Let us consider, then, the several sources of information which are available (see Figure 3.2).

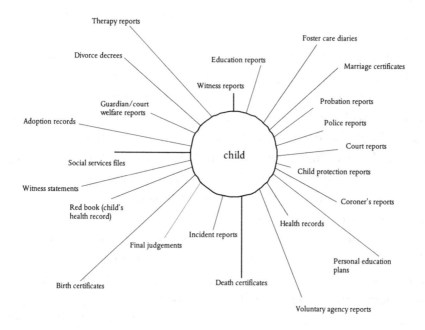

Figure 3.2 Documents available to help construct a child's life story

Confidential and sensitive information

Sensitive material may be held in a number of places, and there are varying ways of obtaining it. An important fact to bear in mind here is the position of the statutory worker, whose authority has parental responsibility for a child, and other workers. The statutory worker will have access to material that will be denied to others.

There are other professionals who will have their own documents. These will be people such as, for example, the family doctor, the health visitor police or officers of the court. A worker who is not a statutory worker will have to demonstrate his need for the material which is sought. If the worker is not successful in this, then he could attempt to obtain the information from the case holder in the social services department because the information will also be held there. If this fails, then parental permission could be sought. However, this may not always be persuasive: a GP, for example, may regard his patient as the child (as opposed to, say, the parent or the local authority acting *in loco parentis*) and will see that it is the child to whom he owes the responsibility for confidentiality.

Medical records cover many kinds of record – those of hospitals and family doctors; psychological and psychiatric reports; the records of child and adolescent mental health teams; and others. To obtain these, the worker will need to demonstrate why it is in the child's best interests that he should be able to consult them. However, coroners' records are public and other kinds of medical record lodged with the coroner may be obtained through that route. Parents, too, may have copies of records and other documents which have been sent to them and they may be willing to make them available.

There is no right to view police witness statements or those of the criminal and civil courts, court judgements or reports ordered by the courts unless party to the proceedings. However, sometimes copies of these documents will be in the files of the social services department and permission will have to be sought to view them. Where they are not, or where the department will not make them available, the department could be asked to act on behalf of the worker's agency to obtain leave of court for such documents to be made available.

Police records can be particularly helpful for two reasons. First, they offer more than a record as they also state conclusions – a belief in what occured. Second, they can lead the worker to other people because the names of witnesses will be noted. Under current law only persons with proper authorization or authority can access criminal records.

Domestic violence units hold records, and many children will have mothers with whom the units have been involved.

A crucial element in the obtaining of documentary information – as with interviewing (see Chapter 4) – is confidentiality. This may be required in seeking the help of fellow professionals, whose willingness to make material available may be a matter of professional discretion – one GP being helpful does not mean that another one will be. The request for information, as we have said, should be based on the best interests of the child, but professionals and others holding information may seek assurances that the information will not be passed on indiscriminately to the child or to others. Workers will need to consider their reaction to such requests according to individual circumstances. As a general rule, though, the worker should be able to offer confidentiality to individuals and professionals, unless the information to be offered concerns a risk to the child. The person being interviewed should be told that information may be shared with the child but that documents will not. However, if information is disclosed about hitherto unknown past abuse, the duty of the worker is to make this known to the social services department.

Public records

The registrar's records are public and as such can be obtained by anyone without any reason given. They include the registers of births, deaths and marriages. These are held at the local register office as well as centrally at the Family Records Centre, London. Wills, too, can be obtained in this way but are held centrally, as are divorce decrees. Only the most minimal information is needed to obtain these central and locally held records.

Newspapers, local and regional newspapers especially, can be helpful in revealing some aspect of a child's life – from a photograph at a school or other functions to a court report. Importantly, newspaper stories may be positive, for example, if a child has taken part in a school drama production, been a member of a sports team, or met a well-known visitor to a school. Children tend, too, to believe what they read, and so newspapers can be important in both filling in gaps or correcting wrong impressions. Newspaper back numbers can be consulted at the offices of the publishers or at the British Library's Newspaper Library at Colindale, north London, and local newspapers can also be seen on microfiche in local libraries.

Information and leads in helping to find people can be obtained through the computerized BT directory inquiry service; business records at Companies House, London; and electoral rolls at local authority offices and local libraries; in addition to wills, other family documents are available at the Family Records Centre, London. The comprehensive website www.192.com relies on telephone directories and electoral rolls so it is very good at locating where people are living.

Children from overseas and from different cultures

The sources of information discussed above will be of assistance for the majority of children for whom life story work is necessary. However, there will be children, like those who are asylum seekers and those who were born overseas, where some of the sources which we have just quoted will not help. Asylum-seeking children, in particular, may have very few possessions and even fewer which throw any light on the information required. They may have come to this country unaccompanied, and so even their parents or other relatives cannot be a source. The countries from which they have come may have experienced civil turmoil, and so records may have been destroyed. Some will come from a culture where great stress is placed on written records, but this may not always be so. In such cases, as with any children from overseas, International Social Services, as already noted, operates a family tracing service. The Red Cross, too, can offer help in countries where there has been civil strife. Contact can also be made with British embassies overseas. But when matters of culture and religion arise, their own embassies in the UK may be a helpful source of information about national life, culture and religion, which could form part of the life story book.

Life story workers and those gathering information should be aware of the way people from different cultures refer to themselves and others. 'Cousin' may not mean what it tends to mean in most European cultures (the son or daughter of one's aunt or uncle), but rather someone much more distantly related, a kinsman or a cousin two or three times removed. Nevertheless this 'cousin' may have a much closer relationship with the child than many Europeans (or certainly white British people) enjoy with their cousins.

Names may not have the same formulations as in some European cultures where the forename comes first and the surname or family name second. Naming in some cultures may also offer clues, for example, as in Ireland where the first grandchild may often have the same first name as a grandparent of the same gender.

Smaller religious groups, like, say, the Plymouth Brethren or the Mormons within Christianity, may have practices which may impede or help information gathering. Mormons, for example, place great emphasis on genealogy, believing that everyone is related by virtue of, literally, being descended from Adam and Eve. It is they who are responsible for the extensive collection of family records, arranged not by name, but by country, which are now freely available in public offices, such as the Family Records Centre, London.

When it comes to questioning relatives, researchers will need to be mindful of to whom it is considered appropriate to talk. For example, in some cultures or even within some smaller Christian sects, addressing women directly is frowned upon.

Exercises

1. Draw your family tree of four generations and identify those individuals that you know least about. List ways in which you can gather information to complete your tree.

2. Create a map for yourself (as in Figures 3.1 and 3.2) to establish the various individuals and documents that would assist an understanding about your life.

3. Consider your childhood memories and identify particular areas of your life of which you have vague or no memory and how you may gather information to enhance your understanding.

4. If someone wanted to trace your school years, whom would they need to contact?

CHAPTER 4

Interviewing
Art not Science

Thinking about whom to interview

All of us are shaped by the people we know in our lives. In our early years this tends to be our parents and other family members, neighbours, friends and friends of the family, and teachers. This is no less so for children who have been traumatized. The difference for them is that some, even many, of those whom they have known will have harmed them instead of helping them to grow healthily or influencing them positively. Also, as a result of this, a veritable army of other people have come into their lives – among them social workers, residential workers, therapists, foster carers, the police, and medical and nursing staff. These people may have been a fleeting presence in a child's life or a more permanent one. A child may, for example, live in one foster home for, say, three years, but may not be able to remember all those professionals who have had an effect on her life. All of these people will have something to say that will shape the life story book and help a child better understand her experiences.

But whom should we interview? One way of deciding this is to draw an ecomap. Here the child will be in the middle and panning out from her will be all the people associated with her. Informing this will be a chronology to show who was where at what time – a very useful tool to guide the interviewer in whom to interview about what. But a key question is, in considering all these people: is there enough information available to warrant an interview at this stage?

As we have just stated, there are many people in the life of a traumatized child. For the purposes of the interview we could categorize them as interventionists (for example, teachers, foster carers, social workers and medical staff) and other people (for example, parents, abusers and those with responsibility of some kind). All the people referred to are very different and each of them will have a different way of responding: some will be sympathetic to the work which is being done, others less so, not least because they feel that they have something to hide or they do not wish to incriminate themselves or others.

It may not always be easy to make contact with some people. Some local authorities, for example, are very reluctant for birth parents to be involved in life story work, and some have refused permission for them to be seen because they know that their own professional practice may not have been of the best. They sometimes believe that, despite all the assurances to the contrary, somehow or other a birth parent will find out where the child is living. If there are child safety concerns, SACCS workers never reveal where they work or give contact information. (This is always the case when visiting prisoners.) Social services departments may also be wary of what the interviewer will discuss with the birth parent.

The whole truth?

If such obstacles cannot be overcome, it can cause gaps in the story; but this itself is part of the story, just as there may be other gaps which tell something. For example, with regard to documentary evidence, the blank space where the father's name should be on the birth certificate is also the story of why it is not there.

Interviewing is not a search for an objective truth (even supposing that that could be discovered). It is more a matter of hearing everyone's story. While all stories tend to be mixtures of fact, fantasy, fiction and wishful thinking, each can offer a fragment of the truth because each person is telling what *they* believe happened. We should be mindful of this whoever is interviewed – it is too easy to imagine that parents and abusers who are not parents will be offering a less true story than, say, foster carers or social workers. This is not necessarily so.

In life story work we should tend to accept what people tell us: we are not there to judge them. Nor are we there to decide what is true or false and possibly, therefore, to dismiss what we have been told. The worker is there to listen, collate and understand the perceptions of those we are interviewing. This will often allow parents to tell of their own failings in a different light. They are being freed to say what they want, to say what they believe happened. In the case example, 'Cary and Vicki: The meaning of water', Michelle would not tell the court that her stepfather was abusing her children because he may then have become abusive towards her. Another woman, physically abused by her husband, had said to him: 'Hit her [their child] – I have had enough.' She would not have said that in court because possible prosecution may have ensued.

Cary and Vicky: The meaning of water

Michelle lived in the north west of England with her two daughters, Cary, aged 12 and Vicky, age nine, and her new partner. Both girls, once placed with SACCS, began to show highly eroticized behaviour when they had any contact with water, even a tap running. There was no obvious reason for this.

In the course of an interview Michelle revealed that her stepfather used to take the girls swimming at what had been, until she moved house, her local pool. In the past he had indecently assaulted Michelle. She did not know what had happened at the pool, but both girls were reluctant to continue to go there with their step-grandfather. However, Michelle continued to let them go because she felt that she had no power to do otherwise. She feared that if she reported her fears, her children could be taken into care and she herself then might be abused again by her stepfather or become alienated from her mother.

However, in a life story interview, she admitted what she had done and so confirmed the child's belief in what had happened.

The child should be told who said what, rather than be given a summary of everything that has been said. She needs to know what someone *said* happened even if that is not factually correct. This is important, too, as it helps to expose the child's confusion rather than to confirm the confusion she feels.

Preparing for an interview

Before the interviewer even goes to the interview he should include within the plan some very basic matters related to risk and health and safety procedures. For example, he should ensure that someone knows where they are. This affords protection both for the interviewer and the interviewee. The interviewer should also telephone the office when the interview is over and say that he has left. If the interview is some distance away and held, say, over two days, he should telephone the office at the end of each day.

The interviewer should also think about a neutral environment because, for example, for some people a social services office will not be helpful because it will bring back the wrong sort of memories. It is also the kind of venue that does not make it easy for interviewees to end the interview if they wish to do so. It is often preferable to meet family members or foster carers in their own homes, because this allows the worker to use his senses and then to refer to what he can see, hear and smell in the environment the child may have lived in. Meeting in this way also allows the interviewee to feel comfortable in their own sur-roundings, but it must be borne in mind that any visit to a family home needs to be considered for possible risk.

It is always preferable for two people to attend an interview. It should then be decided who is to be the note taker and who is to ask the questions. It should be agreed that, other than in extreme circumstances, the person taking notes should not take part in the interview or interrupt his colleague or respond to questions asked of his colleague by the person being interviewed. This is because some people may attempt to manipulate the interview by answering one person's question and not the other's; or they may focus on one interviewer and not the other to avoid answering some questions. It is perfectly acceptable to give the note taker an opportunity to ask relevant questions before ending the interview, but the lead interviewer must be seen to be in this role, and must be the person who concludes the interview.

The interviewer should have in mind the time he thinks the interview will last but should add to this another hour to allow for settling into the interview and for adequate time to be allowed for the 'Colombo' question or the door handle question (see below).

Perhaps the most basic thing of all by way of preliminaries is to make sure how to get to the venue in order not to be late.

As we have said, all the people we have mentioned above who have had an impact on the child's life are very different, with different perspectives and different – sometimes opposing – places in the child's life. But all of them can be approached initially by using techniques which most of us commonly employ when we meet someone we do not know.

Techniques for interviewers

The rapport stage

This is the stage when we want to reassure those whom we want to interview, to allay any fears or misapprehensions they may have and help them to feel at ease in our company and with our questions.

Thus, in this stage we will want to gauge the person to whom we are talking to try to assess his skills and intellectual capacity. How does he deal with someone he has never met before? Is he innately suspicious? Does he simply seek reassurance? What we want to do is to communicate to the interviewee that we are interested in him, that what he has to say is important to us, which itself is a way of assuring him that he is important and that we value him.

The first rule at this stage, on meeting the interviewee, is to talk about everything but the subject to hand! Give him the chance to talk about himself. We might discuss our journey, the weather, where we are meeting him (if it is in his own home this will afford ample opportunity for him to tell us about himself). At this time, too, we need to take account of the environment – Is the television left on? Is there loud music? Are there other adults about? Are there children around? Very often photographs of family members, children long since removed from the interviewee's care, or deceased grandparents, will afford the person the opportunity to discuss and reminisce about those things important to him. One woman visited for a life story interview had very obviously spent a lot of time collecting together and collating photographs because she had a pile of them available when the interviewer arrived. This was her way of entering into the discussion and prompting what she could remember.

Whatever is said to us, no matter how trivial it is or how unrelated it is to the reason why we are actually there, the interviewer should show that he is interested and that he is listening, and not that he is just coming in to the person's life for the interview, carrying it out and moving on, as if it were some mechanical process.

Rapport can also be about language. How articulate is the person? Is English the first language? If it is not, would it be more comfortable, when it comes to the actual interview, to have an interpreter present?

It is important to know if the interviewee has a hearing problem. One life story worker went to see an older married couple where the man was very quick to assume all kinds of things about the visit, about which he needed reassuring. The conversation continued and then the man said that he needed to correct his wife's hearing aid which was not working. Had he not had the reassurance, he would not have done that and what she had to say would never have been said.

The most important impression to be relayed is that the interviewee is a person and we are interested in what he has to say. We are not there to judge him but only to listen and record. In the very act of being listened to many family members, especially parents, have the opportunity to speak about their accountability, their hopes and their fears. This may be the first time that they have been able to do this as, for various reasons, the court process does not allow this: it is adversarial; the person will be led through his evidence; and he may also be advised that some state-ments will be prejudicial to his case.

The contract stage

This follows the rapport stage and is where, having established with the person why we are there, we agree the parameters of the interview. We make sure that interviewer and interviewee understand them. There are approaches to take and not to take. For example, a question like: 'How long have I got?' may elicit the answer: 'An hour'. But if the question is: 'What's your timetable for today?', that may well provoke the response: 'I've nothing much on – I can talk to you for as long as you like.'

In the contract stage, too, the interviewer should explain what he means by confidentiality, that is, what he is told will be confidential except that the interviewer has a duty to report anything affecting the safety of the child. If information is given that would be useful to a third party, then that will be discussed with the interviewee. If anything is to be said which the interviewee would prefer was not to be shared with the child, then that, too, is something which will be discussed.

The interviewer should also make it clear that the interviewee can choose to keep whatever he wishes to himself and also that he knows that he can stop the interview if he wants. But it is also important that the person being interviewed knows that any information will be used professionally, sensibly and sensitively. This means ensuring that parents know that painful information they give the worker will be imparted appropriately to the child. For example, a parent may disclose (possibly for the first time) that he was himself abused as a child and say that he does not want his child to know that. What this usually means is that they do not want the information to be put as brutally as they have imparted it. The worker should explain that he will say to the child something like: 'Your daddy was hurt in a sex way and that's the cause of his muddles'; or 'Your daddy's daddy could not keep him safe when he was little.' Rape can be expressed as 'Mum had sex when she didn't want to have sex'. Few children are surprised at this information.

But those who have abused and may have been themselves abused may well deny any responsibility (even when criminally convicted), may blame everyone but themselves (even the child), and be manipulative. They may claim that they told the social services department about the child's sexualized behaviour or that what had happened had occurred at the nursery school and not at home. They may attempt to justify physical abuse on the basis of the child's own allegedly disruptive behaviour. There are ways of confronting abusers with the truth, for example by quoting other statements or medical reports. But if a parent is denying it, it is the parent's story, even if it is not what was understood as true. However, if the parent persists then the story along with other (conflicting) accounts can be presented to the child. Children can get angry at their parents' accounts about what happened to them and this can be a trigger for the child giving more information and exploring what else she remembers. It may well be, for example, that the child will show that the mother was more involved than social services realized.

Another part of the contract stage is about how the interview will be recorded. It is better not to use a tape recorder. This can be intimidating to the interviewee; it can distract the interviewer who may be concerned if it is working correctly; and if the tape breaks or the machine breaks down then everything will be lost. It is also the case that life story work takes time, and the time that is required to transcribe an interview of perhaps two or three hours when a verbatim interview is not required is not time well spent. An hour-long interview, typically, can be transcribed into 6000 words.

It is much better to take notes, but it should be established, first of all, if note taking is acceptable to the person being interviewed. If there are two people meeting the interviewee, then it is best to decide before the meeting who is to be the note taker. The interviewee should also be offered a copy of the note of the meeting. If he cannot read or cannot read English, then he should have the chance to name someone – a family friend, a solicitor, an interpreter – to whom the notes can be sent. Making the notes available also makes the interviewer accountable.

The interviewer should also explain that he cannot give detailed information about the child – where the child is living or who cares for her – but information can be given about how she is.

When the contract has been established, the interviewer should confirm that what has been agreed is acceptable and ask if there is any more which the interviewee wants to say at this stage.

Free narrative

This is the technique by which the interviewer encourages the person being interviewed to say what he wants without being circumscribed by detailed questions.

Interviewers should not arrive with a set of questions to which they are determined to have the answers by the time they leave. This would restrict what may be revealed – the unexpected, the unknown – but the encounter underlines a power imbalance that can lead to essential information not being revealed. A conversational interview is likely to reveal more, as well as diminishing the inequality of the meeting. Using set questions also means that the interviewer can be distracted by being determined to go from one question to the next until he reaches the last one. This will lead to him not listening as well as he should and not picking up what is being said, and it will cause him to go along routes where the questions take him, rather than where the answers from the interviewee may lead – and these may not be the most fruitful routes to follow. However, interviewers should always bear in mind the word 'What?' It is with 'What?' that they should begin each question. This is because it is an information-seeking question. After this the 'Why?', 'Where?', 'When?', 'Who?' and 'How?' questions can be used to elaborate on the answers.

When considering the first words of a question regarding an event or an incident, it is useful to identify the insinuated meaning behind each one: 'What?' asks for details; 'Where?' asks for location; 'When?' asks for the time frame; 'Who?' asks for the identity of the people present; and 'How?' asks for the mechanics of the event or incident. 'Why?' is perhaps the most ill-used beginning of any question in these interviews because it demands justification, often personal, and carries a suggestion of blame. In sensitive interviews 'Why?' is to be avoided in order to ensure the non-judgemental manner in which the interview is conducted. In many situations, the 'Why?' can be replaced with 'What?'; for example 'Why did you do that?' could be rephrased as 'What reasons do you feel there are for the actions taken?'

Thus, questions have to be as open as possible. It is very easy to assume that what we have in mind, what we want to find out is all that the person can usefully tell us. This is not so. It is also the fact that someone who may be wary of saying too much may welcome detailed questions: it is very easy to answer the questions asked and not tell what one is reluctant to tell and is not questioned about.

A very open question can be: 'What do you want to tell me?' The answer may take two minutes or two hours – the listening skills required to deal with the response to such a question are immense, and even note taking can be a distraction. (The experienced interviewer may very well come to realize that he develops an ability to recall the critical parts of answers without taking notes.)

Listening is a skill, because how many people hear but do not listen? Listening is about calculated silences; it is about eye contact, body language and posture. It is about the fruitful offering of a 'Yes', a nod or some other gesture every now and again. These assure the interviewee of our continuing interest without distracting him or interrupting what he has to say. (It should be noted that silences, eye contact and body language and the way words are used are as useful to the interviewee in understanding the interviewer as vice versa.)

But while the aim is to let the person talk, there is also a skill in knowing how to stop an interviewee from going around in circles or being repetitive. Sometimes a detailed question will have to be asked, in order to get the person back on track.

When the possibilities of free narrative have been exhausted, open questions will cease.

Confirmation

This stage is the summary of the salient points which the interviewee has made in response to the initial questions. These pomits may themselves lead the interviewer to ask further questions.

John and Michael: The witch and the poison

John and Michael were two brothers, aged five and two. It had been decided that they had suffered harm and neglect in the care of their mother and then their grandmother, where the social services department had placed them. They were then placed in a foster home, where the boys believed that they would be abused again. They believed that the foster carer was a witch who could use magic to harm them.

Of the incident described, all that either remembers is that Michael fell down the stairs and through a glass window. John convinced Michael that he had been 'magicked there' by the foster carer who he said was a witch, a view with which Michael concurred. Neither remembered the foster carer being present when the incident happened. The foster carer remembered Michael going through the window but not falling down the stairs.

She was asked to tell her story from the point when she heard the glass smash. She remembered walking down the stairs and that the safety gate at the top was open. She then remembered (which she had not done before) that she had left it open. As a result of her remembering, she felt a responsibility for the accident which she had never felt before. In turn, this provoked questions about care, support and supervision of the children.

The belief that the foster carer, a single woman, was a witch continued to the extent that John, fearing that she would poison them, used to taste his food and Michael's. He would also 'save' Michael by sometimes jumping in his way to protect him from some imagined harm which the foster carer would 'magic'.

The boys were moved to a new fostered home. When the woman died of cancer, John believed that had caused this so he and his brother could be moved because he had believed, without any evidence, that he was being abused in this foster home, too, because all the women – his mother, grandmother, the single foster carer and the carer who had died – were in some way involved in a conspiracy to harm him and his brother.

It was only after life story work, therapy, and therapeutic parenting[7] that the boys knew that they were not being poisoned, that the accident with the gate was, in fact, an accident caused by the foster carer's neglect and that there was no conspiracy to abuse them. In the same way, the boys knew that they did not cause the death of the foster carer through magic.

Rainbow questions

These are so called because just as the colours of the rainbow shade into each other at the edges, so the answer to one question can lead to another being asked – and there may be a pot of gold at the end!

This is where we look at historical issues to elicit information that may need some kind of prompting through a mental association by the person interviewed. He needs to be asked what he saw or how he felt or what he sensed in certain situations. We need this in some detail because first impressions are very important, and in life story work it is critical to know how an adult responded to a child – positively and negatively – and to attempt to offer the child some knowledge of what *did* happen at a certain time and not what he *thinks* happened. We may be able to relay to the child some details like a smell or a sight that may have significance for her in dredging up a memory that places her back in time.

For example, if a foster carer is asked what a child was like when she came into the house, the person may say that the child was crying and bedraggled and carrying two bin liners containing her possessions. But if it is found out that, say, it was raining or in the middle of the night, that the radio was on or that music was playing loudly upstairs or that the smell of the evening meal was wafting into the hallway, these will be much better triggers or scene setters for a child who is wanting to go back and find out about her past. It is details like these that can cause memories to come flooding back.

In such cases foster carers, for example, could be asked to close their eyes and place themselves back in the time when the child arrived. They would then be asked to take the interviewer, step by step, from the time of arrival to the child's bedtime. Once this is done the interviewer could reflect with them on a particular part of that period, such as mealtime or reading a bedtime story that day. This allows the interviewer to have a clearer view of what the child was like – for example, was she used to having a story read to her or had she herself cleaned her teeth before?

Just as people will sometimes exaggerate, so they will telescope their memories to very basic facts in order to minimize what has happened or shift the blame onto someone else. It is the rainbow questions which allow the fuller picture to emerge.

Although we have referred to the interview process in stages, this should not be dogmatically adhered to – it may be useful sometimes to go back from rainbow questions to the free narrative.

Closed questions

These are related to confirmation. Here the interviewee is asked very specifically if a statement he made was correct ('You told me this – is it correct?'). This is not about the truth or doubting his word, but to confirm his view of what happened, and this should be made plain. It

Tom: Blood and water

Tom, aged five, developed a phobia about splashes of water, which then grew to be a fear of water. His mother had seriously attacked his father, and it was known that Tom had seen his father's severely injured body. But what was not known, until his mother was interviewed, was that Tom had actually witnessed the attack. His mother had stabbed his father so severely that blood had spurted everywhere, and he came to associate the spurting and flow of blood with the pouring and running of water. No one had made this connection previously because no one had known that Tom had witnessed the attack.

may not have happened but that does not mean that the person is lying; he simply believes that something occurred in a certain way. However, if the person says it is incorrect, he should not be challenged by saying something like: 'But you told me that'. He should be asked what did happen. He can then set the record straight without being accused of fabricating a story.

The summary

This is where a summary of the person's experience of, and with, the child from all that he has said is presented to him.

The Colombo question

This is linked to the summary and is named after the television detective who always seemed to have finished questioning his suspects and then, as he was leaving, would put his finger to his brow and say: 'Just one more question.' This is the other side of the coin to what social workers call the 'door handle question', the question which the person interviewed often asks just as the interviewer has his hand on the door handle ready to leave. These can range from 'Can I see my child?' to 'I haven't told you about…' or 'You haven't asked me about…'.

The Colombo question is a double-edged one and can be something like: 'Lots of children talk about the best and the worst times in their lives. Can you think back – what was yours?' or: 'Can I ask this? You have mentioned your social worker on a number of occasions but what do you really think of her?' or: 'Would it be ok for me to meet your current partner [or previous one, if relevant]?'

These questions are asked at this point because they were not relevant in the context of earlier questions and were certainly too detailed to provoke the free narrative. However, they are relevant in the context of what has been said. Sometimes such questions can be asked quite casually as if prompted by pictures or objects in the room.

The summary and the Colombo questions may seem to bring everything to a close. However, what we have described is a thought-out process and so it must have an ending.

The ending

There is no need now to go back over what has been said: now the intention is to ensure that what has happened has been acceptable and that the interviewee is ok. If the interviewee is suffering any distress, then it is necessary to make sure that he has someone to whom he can turn. This could be a friend nearby or – where some past assault has been disclosed – advice that there are places of support such as a rape crisis centre, the family doctor or a survivors' group.

The interviewer should finish by thanking the person for seeing him and for the information given. The interviewer should repeat that he has not been there to judge and does not intend to do so as a result of anything which has been said.

What can be gained and what could be lost

What an interview produces is information of many kinds. One of the most useful is the anecdote, because that tells the story around an event that may be, at best, dry without it or, at worst, meaningless. It may explain hitherto puzzling information and may also inject some humour (see the case example below).

Tina: The baby in a bucket

Tina was 19 and did not know she was pregnant. She was visiting her mother's house and wanted to go the toilet because she had a stomach ache. The toilet was outside and so her mother gave her a bucket to use in the house to save her going outside, as was the family's practice. When she sat over the bucket, she gave birth to Grant. He was born there because there was nowhere else for him to be delivered. This helped to explain why the address on Grant's birth certificate was different from the one at which his mother was living. This also offered an interesting story to share with him in his life story work.

Anecdotes are part of everyone's inheritance, and for children whose childhoods have been so disturbed and fractured they take on an added importance. For such children, too, in addition to the common or garden anecdotes of family life – the first day at school, the wedding, how parents met, the chaos of holidays – there are others to be recorded about social workers, going into care, arrival at a foster home. Some will be sad, but some will also be joyous or funny. Most anecdotes tend to have a positive meaning for families and are important to individuals as they struggle through life. Even the anecdotes about a family tragedy, say, the death of a father, will give some impression of what kind of man he was.

The essential thing about the interviewer is his neutrality, objectivity and lack of judgementalism. He is the receptacle for what is said to him. Leading questions are the bugbear of social work interviewing and can stem from the inequality between interviewer and the person interviewed. Hamlet asks Polonius: 'Do you see yonder cloud that's almost in shape of a camel?' and the conversation continues:

Polonius:	By the mass, and 'tis like a camel, indeed.
Hamlet:	Methinks it is like a weasel.
Polonius:	It is backed like a weasel.
Hamlet:	Or like a whale?
Polonius:	Very like a whale.

Polonius will not disagree because Hamlet is the prince; power resides in him. Interviewers should not go to the interview seeking answers to confirm their preconceptions or looking for evidence to fit a diagnosis. It is entirely possible for an interviewer to manipulate the interview to obtain information that he requires to fit a particular theory or understanding. To do this would be to devalue the exercise and to impart to the child misrepresentations which themselves may serve to further confuse the child and her story. Doing this serves neither party – nor, least of all, the child.

Exercises

1. As an exercise for two people, select a subject to discuss – for example, the last holiday, weekend activities – and spend ten minutes talking to your partner. Consider the words you use when you begin each question, and at the end of the exercise reflect on the difference of quality in the response.

2. Consider your own professional and personal values in relation to acquiring information about people who sometimes are unaware that you have obtained it. An example of this may be obtaining birth records of adults who are unaware that this is being done. This is similar to making use of social work files of whose existence or content service users are unaware.

3. Do you consider it acceptable to discuss with a child her life stories without giving opportunities to family members to share their understanding of events to which they have been party?

4. Think of a child of whom you are aware who is not known to social services. Using a sheet of paper write their name in the middle and circle it. Then identify all those individuals and organizations that impact on this child's life. This process should demonstrate the number of individuals who affect children every day of their lives.

CHAPTER 5

Safe at Last
Providing a Safe and Stable Environment

Comfort and distress

It is an axiom of good parenting that a newborn baby thrives when she feels safe and secure. This happens in many ways – by being held securely, spoken to often and gently, guarded from shock and too much noise, kept in a warm and clean place – it may be her cot, it may be her pram – which is soft and protective. In short, when new parents do this, they are showing one aspect of the love which they feel for their child and in doing so provide a secure base for the child's exploration and growth. As part of this the baby expresses her needs, and learns to trust her caregivers if these needs are met. This, in turn, leads the baby to feel that her needs are acceptable and that she is herself worthwhile; she feels safe and protected and that generally the world is ok. From this position of security she feels able to begin to explore the external world and develop a sense of independence and identity.

Few traumatized children will have known such loving kindness, care, attention and all-enveloping security. For them the world which they explore is a very different place: cruel, harsh, violent; a place of fear and hurt. Physical violence and verbal and sexual abuse, as a victim or as a witness, or very likely both, creates an atmosphere that teaches the child that the approach of an adult is more likely to be a threat than a comfort. Added to this, such children often grown up in unkempt homes in areas or on estates where they have to learn from an early age to watch out for themselves, where contact with many adults and some children and young people is no escape from the negative atmosphere of home.

Thus, the child who comes into care has to learn that adults can be a comfort, can offer security and safety, can love and are most definitely not like the adults whom she has hitherto known. That is a general principle of working with children in care. It is no less so when it comes to life story work. Whatever impacts on the child – social, physical and emotional – must all be based on safety. The child must never be placed in a situation, when the work is being carried out, where she is in any risk.

Social, physical and emotional risk

Let us look at those three areas where risk must be guarded against: social, physical and emotional. With regard to the first – social – this applies to the people whom children meet. They must not be brought in contact with anyone who might cause them harm – especially those who may have caused them harm in the past where they are able to repeat such harm. There is also the question of the 'internal' environment so that play is safe – this means children not playing with one another in a room in the home without an adult being aware of this; not playing in, say, the garden unsupervized when there is a chance that they may exhibit unsafe behaviour – possibly, behaviour which is sexualized or which may be physically dangerous.

Children whose behaviour is complex and very difficult may, because of past experiences, have a very skewed and perhaps damaging understanding of sex, love, warmth and comfort. A child like this who says that she likes another child may express this emotion in the only way in which she knows how – the only way she has been brought up to do – and that is sexually.

Jamie: The father as hero

Jamie was ten and knew that his father had committed suicide, but no one had told him how he had died or talked to Jamie about his own feelings. It was clear from information gathering that he had been given different versions of his father's death from foster carers, as well as social workers: his father had cut his wrists, taken an overdose, hanged himself. Jamie's mother, Eileen, was asked how her husband had died and she said that he had hanged himself. She produced a copy of the death certificate.

Jamie's father, James, had been a successful civil engineer. When working at a power station he had met his future wife. She came from a fragmented and dysfunctional family. James's parents opposed the marriage, and when it went ahead disowned their son. The marriage, which produced Jamie, was brief and passionate; within a year the couple were divorced. Eileen felt guilty for what happened.

While Jamie continued to live with his mother in the north east of England, his father got a job on a construction project in London but continued to travel each week to see his son. Eileen had, however, found herself a new partner, a man with whom she had two children but also someone who abused her and also abused Jamie.

James was devastated by both the loss of his son and the disowning by his parents. He met an Irishwoman and they decided to marry. But, travelling to Ireland to inform her parents, she never returned. Then the company for whom James was working went bankrupt without paying him. He took his own life.

The three versions of his father's death confused Jamie. To him James was a hero, because to him his mother, whom he intensely disliked, had left his father and was the cause of his problems, whereas his father had never harmed him. James coming at weekends to take Jamie out seemed almost to Jamie to be a rescue from the home he disliked. In his mind there was an element of heroic self-sacrifice about his father's life, which he could too easily come to imitate. This needed to be avoided by his coming to realize why people act as they do. This meant that James had to be knocked off the pedestal where he had been placed by Jamie, but without being destroyed in Jamie's eyes.

The various versions about the way in which James had taken his life were due to poor record keeping and poor communication between successive carers and the local authority into whose care Jamie was taken. This was exacerbated by the fact that Jamie went through many placements, some lasting only days. In one he had pulled a knife on the foster carer.

Jamie became acquainted with the facts of his father's life, rather than his fantasy about his father, by a physical journey. He went back to where he had been born; he visited the power station where his father had worked; he returned to one of his placements; and saw the women's refuge where his mother had taken him to escape from Jamie's abusive stepfather. He also saw where his father had worked in London and the house where he lived when working there, as well as the house where he had died.

In doing all this, Jamie had to feel safe with his life story worker and also with the two key carers, each of whom accompanied Jamie and the life story worker on different parts of the journey. Jamie had to be with people he had come to know and whom he knew would look after him. This was because what he had assumed about his father – his heroic status, the confused stories about his death – were now being tested. This could lead to difficult reactions – emotional and tearful, withdrawal – but however Jamie was to express it, he had to know that he could do so in safety. Eventually, he was able to do so.

In life story work what is being teased out are the child's memories, distortions, beliefs and fears. When this is explored, it brings with it a series of behaviours as the child tries to work out what all of this means. The life story worker observes and interviews. He provides safety for the child to allow her to explore her life and unhappiness.

A child can be told by the worker that she is safe and that the worker can be trusted. But why should the child believe this when what has gone before, what she has seen or experienced is the opposite – adults who abuse trust, who create places where the child has felt anything but safe. Unless a child can come to see that she is safe, that the worker can be trusted, then attempts to undertake life story work will be futile. An important part of the work is that children feel able to take risks while feeling safe. When physically exploring children's lives with them – often away from the residential home in the outside world, maybe in places where she has lived – rather than instructing them what will be done, they can be asked what they want to do. Who do they want to do it with? Where do they want to go and who with? This does not of itself say to children that they are safe, but it allows them to make decisions – their decisions – knowing that they have been involved in the arrangements. They may, for example, know that they can risk going around the rundown estate, with its boarded-up houses, where they lived, because they have made a decision to do so with someone whom they have chosen. They have not been forced to do so.

Children can carry over their feeling of being unsafe into what everyone else knows is a safe environment. For example, one boy in a residential home never opened his curtains, yet outside he could have seen woods, fields and sheep grazing. The life story worker, who did not know about this, visited the area in which he had lived and discussed it with the boy's key carer. The area was known for all too obvious reasons as 'Little Beirut'. The life story worker gained entry to the block of flats where the boy had lived and, looking out, saw what the boy would have seen from his bedroom window – burned out cars, mattresses and other rubbish piled up in a glass-strewn courtyard. But only when the life story worker discussed this with the boy's key carer, who alone knew about the closed curtains, did the boy's need to keep his view obscured make sense.

When it comes to ensuring a child's safety, there are certain practical considerations to bear in mind. For example, when returning to a home area, don't go in the school holidays. There may be children about whom the child knows and whose association with her may have been

Ceri: A chance meeting

Ceri was 14 when she was visiting an area where she had been fostered, about which she claimed to remember hardly anything. As she was driven around the area, she spotted one of her former foster carers working in his front garden. She said that she wanted to meet him again. The life story worker had to make sure if he was, indeed, who Ceri said he was and, if so, to explain the problem of her seeing him again, which revolved around matters unsettled from when she left his care. There was also the question of whether it was advisable to allow a visit for which no preparation had been made.

The worker left the car, walked back to where the man was, spoke to him and established that he had been the carer. The man said that he would get his wife, who was inside their house. It was agreed that Ceri could come and meet them for five minutes, provided the workers were with her at all times. The meeting may only have been for five minutes but for the next hour and a half in the car Ceri, the child who had said that she had no memories of the area, talked continuously about the placement – who her foster carers were, who they knew, the things they did as a family, what it was like living with them.

painful. There are some places that a child simply cannot go back to because there is the possibility of her meeting people who are part of her unhappy past. Such an area could be an estate, a small village or a caravan park.

This doesn't mean that all is lost in gathering information in this way. Not only can the worker continue to look for it but there can be surprises along the way. For example, one life story worker went to a holiday camp that was used, out of season, for housing homeless families. One of the children had at one time lived there. He enquired if anyone remembered the chalets that were used by homeless families. A caretaker was called who had worked there for many years. He knew the chalets and that only one family, that of the child, had lived there. He had many stories to tell without knowing anything about the child cared for by SACCS. The information he offered was clearly about her and contributed towards the life story book.

Safety and security

Linked to safety, but separate from it, is security. This means the child having a secure attachment to a person (see Chapter 1 for a discussion of attachment). Security takes safety a step further. We can make a child safe by our own efforts, which means protecting her, but we cannot offer security: this is something a child needs to feel. Why should it be otherwise? She has been let down every day of her life – there is no reason for her to feel secure because someone tells her that she is. But when a child comes to feel secure it allows her to take risks emotionally, to open up to the worker. Part of this depends, too, on the worker's reaction to what he is told: if he recoils, a child may not say more because she may feel that she is hurting the worker. It is a fact that children, however harmed and having experienced extreme events, will still often choose to protect those around them. It is known from child witness interviews that children will often choose not to state the extent of wrongs perpetrated on them if they are not confident that the adult helping them can deal with the information.

Containment

With safety, too, comes containment. We need to think about all the issues that impinge on this and how we plan to deal with them. This can mean that there are points past which children cannot go, because to do so places them at risk of harm. They need to know that in the exploration and questioning they will become sad or get angry but that they will not be led into areas which are potentially emotionally harmful. Children can receive assurance about this because assurance is a part of feeling safe and secure. However, having a contract that lays down boundaries and rules in creating the life story book can assist this and create responsibility for *all* those involved. Life story is a part of therapy,

Rebecca: The risk of losing everything

Rebecca was nine and had been placed in care because of neglect, along with her sister and two half-sisters. She was aggressive, insulting, used bad language and paid little attention to her personal hygiene. This made her very unpopular in the residential home where she lived, which in itself caused problems in an environment meant to be accepting and nurturing.

When it came to life story work, while Rebecca was very engaged with the process, she also had good and bad days and was testing the adults looking after her to find out whether they liked her only on good days and disliked her on bad days. What she had to learn is that she – like most other people – could not be good all the time, but nor was she bad all the time. She needed to see and experience that life was not, and could not be, perfect.

Rebecca had never spoken of being abused, but there was a suspicion that she had been abused, although there had been no criminal prosecution of an abuser, no unsolicited disclosure and no child protection procedures instituted.

She saw a major risk in disclosing abuse: Would those who were helping her like her if they knew she was abused and acted in a sexual way with others? Would it get her into trouble? Would she be able to continue to live in the home? There were many reasons, in her mind, why she would be better to keep quiet. But she had to be given the opportunity to speak – to have been able to see, in her terms, that she had not failed and that she was safe. It was her realization that she could speak and not lose what she valued by doing so that proved to be the breakthrough.

and therapy is not about creating harm but recovering from it. An example of where life story work could spill over into areas that create harm is where a child is aggressive towards one of her carers outside the boundary of the life story session.

Life story work allows children to explore safely and securely how they have reached where they are and to attach identity and meaning to their lives, to consider, to think, to understand, to reflect. It helps them to rediscover and confirm who they are; to work through the decisions which were made in their interests – for example, why were they placed with one person and why that placement didn't work out. They can ask questions that they might like to have asked at the time had they been able to do so from a position of being safe and feeling secure.

For all of us, taking risks means accepting that we can fail, but most of us can take risks against some sense of security and safety. It is no different for the traumatized child: she must be given the opportunity to feel safe about failing. Children need to understand that they should not feel that they must do what we want them to do or tell us what they think we want to hear. They should be able to be open about their feelings, actions and reactions, about things that they may feel that workers would disapprove of or not countenance as failure. These may be things as various as not winning a race at school, being expelled from school, or behaving in a way which is anti-social. They can be told (perhaps with personal examples) that we all fail in some way and that we have all done things we wish we hadn't done. They need to know that they can fail and still be safe and loved and given the opportunity to succeed.

Listening to children

A key to children having a sense that they are safe and secure is that the worker should ask and listen to them positively. The temptation in life story work is to provide information to children and have them work through it superficially. But the really important thing is to ask them questions; for example, What do they remember about this incident, episode, period or person? How do they feel now about what happened? They can be asked what they think life might or could have been like.

It was said at the beginning of this book that life story work is much more than being about the facts of a child's life, because it accepts the fiction, fantasy and make believe. It is, therefore, critical for the work, but also for the element of safety and security, that children be allowed to state their own memories, which may be faulty or coloured by wishful

Nicola: The realistic view

When 12-year-old Nicola saw her father rape her mother, what she remembered was not the rape but her mother hiding in the corner of the room and wetting herself in fear. Her mother had told what had happened during a life story interview, but rather than Nicola be told the facts, she was asked why she thought her mother was in the corner of the room. What did she think that her mother was feeling? This led on to further discussions with Nicola saying that she thought her father had a right to do what he did because her mother would not let him have sex with her. Nicola had placed her father on a pedestal so that she could justify his actions. She could not make the link between what her father had done and her picture of her mother, afraid, in the corner of the room. Nothing could diminish her father in her eyes. When later she came to talk about her father's abuse of her, she said that she didn't think that he had meant to hurt her and maybe he had done this because of her mother's attitude towards sex or that she, as a four-year-old, wanted him to do these things to her.

She was enabled to see not that her father was necessarily bad but that she had to develop a more realistic view of him and what he did. She was helped to do this by considering the respective heights of the people involved. How high was she? How high was her father? What power did she think she, at her height, could have over her father at his height? She could see the authority of adults and whether children are able to say what they want and what they don't want.

She was then encouraged to talk about rights. What right do people have to do this or that to children? What control do children have? There was no point in telling her that her father was responsible for doing wrong things – many people had told her that. What was needed was what came about: for her to come to see that what he had done caused sadness and harm, and that that was why she could no longer live with her parents.

thinking, and reflect upon them. The life story worker is not saying to the child: 'This is your life' but 'What is your life?'

This can be difficult for both child and worker: it is easy to want to evade some questions or avoid some situations in order to protect the child and save her from distress. The inclination for both worker and child will be, naturally, to accept what is being said, but this does not allow the essential exploring. Even when the facts seem to be to hand, they should be explored, or else how can we really know what children know about significant events in their lives? To take only the facts to be found in social work files is unhelpful, because they tend, for the most part, to be an evidential, critical and selective account of crises and failure and so cannot tell the whole story, however full they may make it appear to be.

If we are to ask, we must listen – not to do the second invalidates the first. Listening means both hearing and not denying the answer. Even if the worker knows that the answer is wrong, he should allow the child to continue because that may reveal how the child arrived at the answer. When the child has finished speaking, the response is not then to state that what has been said is wrong. It will be more useful (having gathered information from elsewhere) to say: 'Would you now like to know what X says?' Offering the alternative statement may lead to further exploration.

An encouragement to children, and a means by which they can come to know that they are safe and secure, is the positive role model presented by their workers, who need to be positive in their outlook. They need to be able to share things about themselves so that the child can see that the worker is willing to be open with them as the worker asks the child to be. This also allows the child to see that the worker is human and that human frailty does not lead to a loss of respect. If the worker is positive, this also allows the child to see that there are people who will offer her praise. And, importantly, children can see that there are adults who have a relationship with them who can act appropriately, showing respect and receiving trust.

Jack: A journey home

Jack was 11 and had suffered years of abuse. He had many bad memories, most of which were factually accurate. He had spent two years working on his life story, and nearing its completion it was decided to take him back to his home area.

His reactions to this would be emotional and unpredictable, even though he had faced many of the demons in his life in producing his book.

The journey from his new home to his old one was a long one. He started out a cheery, open child but as the journey progressed, he seemed almost to shrink physically as he sat in the back of the car.

The first stop was the hospital where he had been born, but he refused to leave the car, even to visit the maternity ward. He looked at the hospital only by standing up and looking through the sunroof of the car. The journey continued, but at none of the other significant places in his life – his nursery school and first foster home – would he get out of the car. But when he arrived at the house where he had been abused, he announced that he wanted to get out of the car and look around. The house was on a rundown estate, and as he walked around, he let go of the hands of the two workers who were accompanying him. Back in the car, the boy who had gone more and more into himself on the journey there, returned to the outgoing child he had been at the start of the journey.

Jack had been able to do what he had done by his own choice. He had tested those who were with him to see if they would push him in any way, but they had not sought to make him leave the car at the hospital or other places when he was reluctant to move. Thus, when he reached the estate he felt able to do what he had come to do there. He felt safe and secure with those who were with him and could say to himself, in the place where he had been abused, that he would not be scared there, he had overcome all that it had represented for him.

Jack's experience shows that safety and security are about both the physical and the emotional.

How time is used is very important. Questioning should never be rushed. The average time to create a life story book is about 12 months – three months to acquire factual information, nine months on the work itself. It will take about 120 hours to complete the whole process and conclude with a life story book.

Consistency is an important virtue: the worker should be punctual and supportive. Children want to know that the life story worker is with them on the journey and that they will stick with it until the end, which will also demand reliability from the worker. Children in care, particularly children who have been traumatized, find it very difficult to deal with unpredictability. Predictability should be a part of the social and physical environment in which the child lives – predictability about going to school with predictable mealtimes and bedtimes. Workers need to be predictable, too. In fact, the more predictable the child sees the worker as being, the more risks the child will feel she can take – and taking risks is a key part of the work. Once risk taking is seen to work, this will assist recovery.

Exercises

1. Think of the last time you felt unsafe and why, and consider what you believed the consequences could be.

2. Consider what safety means to you in three ordinary situations.

3. When you are next in a situation when someone (for example, your partner, a colleague or a friend) is telling you something, reflect on the processes that you have used when listening to them.

4. Consider the last time you took a risk. Was it worth it, and what were the safety nets that you had?

CHAPTER 6

Internalization
Towards an Understanding

Our lives: Knowing and not knowing

Like many of us, traumatized children can know facts about their lives but find it difficult accepting them as their own. Unlike most of the rest of us, though, what they have experienced may make it even more difficult to do so – something, indeed, which may only be possible after years of intensive therapy. This process of acceptance is called internalization.[8] It is an emotional understanding by a child of who she is spiritually, socially, culturally and familially, in terms of attitudes and values – as well as how she has reached where she has in her life. It is the gaining of self-knowledge.

Internalization is the second stage of life story – the first stage of information gathering is about the external story, and the third stage is the production of the life story book.

In helping children to come to this understanding, life story work is critical because it presents not just a factual narrative but also the opportunity for children to explore what has happened to them and why, who the interested parties – for good or bad – were, along with their own histories, and the consequences of actions taken against the child, as well as on the child's behalf. Curiously, Nicholls (2003), writing of life story work with children available for adoption, says it is failing because, among other things, 'it confuses the need for information with the need for direct or therapeutic work'. In fact, as we argue throughout this book, there is no contradiction between the two, indeed the two are a means to the same end: the child's being able to know what happened to her and why is a part of the healing process.

However, it is important to emphasize that neither life story nor internalization is about the retelling of facts: children should be allowed, as far as is practicable, to come to an understanding of them for themselves. This is what we mean by children's exploration: to come to an understanding of an event. Events do not have to be those which the child has experienced or of which they have a memory – it may be something that has happened in the lives of their parents or grandparents. This is about promoting, assisting, supporting (which is much more than allowing) children to explore at their own pace, whatever the issues are – divorce, sex, abuse, birth, violence, death.

Much of this chapter may seem to be more about the mechanics of life story – we explain, for example, about preparation, getting started, how long sessions should last, contracts and so on – and this may seem at first sight to be out of place in a chapter about internalization. But life story and internalization are intimately linked, and life story, a part of therapy, is a way of helping children internalize.

Because children can see their life before them, as well as having the opportunity to revisit places and people significant to them, they know that internalization is not a matter of saying: 'You have dealt with the past and now you can move on to the future', as if the past is something which can be compartmentalized, looked at and then set aside. Rather it is about knowing who they are and being able to embrace the past, learn from it and reflect upon it. It is after that that they can move forward, more securely and confidently.

In more conventional forms of life story work, for example, with children who are being placed for adoption, children will be given facts, shown photographs and other memorabilia of their lives. But what they cannot do is to attach themselves, their inner selves to this. What is important for a child is the story that surrounds the photograph – the biography of the person photographed or their relationship with the

Christina: When death is real

Christina was seven when her ten-day-old sister, who had been born prematurely, and her grandmother, who had a brain haemorrhage, died within days of each other near Christmas. The story that Christina had was that her sister had died in her arms, which may have seemed fanciful or a wish-fulfilment on her part. But the life story worker's investigations turned up a picture of Christina holding her dead sister, and it appeared that while the baby, literally, did not die in her arms she had been allowed to hold the body. Christina's mother had the photograph copied and, if it is felt possible to do so, it may be put in Christina's life story book. The question would be whether it was appropriate to show a picture of a dead child.

child or someone close to the child; what happened in the house in the picture; what the connection was between the father in one photograph and the grandparents in the other. It is as if these facts and mementos are both a part of the child but not a part of the child, thus creating, in her emotions, a bifurcation between her outer and inner lives. Presented as no more than visual facts – 'This is X', 'This is Y' – photographs are drained of life and significance, which is then denied to the child. The child who has no opportunity to explore her own thinking, conceptions and life has her confusion exacerbated and misunderstandings multiplied.

Let us take an all-too-common occurrence for children in care – experiencing multiple placements. If they have not been given the chance to work through what has happened in each placement, why it broke down, why the child has been moved so often, then it is not surprising that that child will have no expectation of the next placement, have no commitment to it, and will believe that she is in some way responsible for the breakdown. The more she is let down, the more she loses of herself; she then becomes even more inward-looking, self-protective and defensive. Without such an opportunity, her own fantasies about what has happened will take on the form of fact. Indeed, a child's memory of events may well, indeed, be accurate, but either people have chosen not to acknowledge that or they have no chance to explore it.

Putting down the wallpaper

The initial recording of the child's story is done, literally, on wallpaper. Wallpaper has many virtues: it is cheap and easily obtained, and it can be rolled up and rolled back and allows the whole story to be recorded continuously (rolls can be added – the average story takes five or six rolls). Sheets of paper or exercise books are good for recording specific subjects, but there can be something symbolic about turning the page and thus turning off or putting something in the past; the sense of continuity can be lost. Wallpaper unravels to show what has happened so far and is, literally, a continuum; it has a visual unity and continuation that the child can see. Wallpaper is also versatile and flexible – it can be drawn and painted on, it can be glued, it can take collage. It is also more difficult to obliterate what has been written or drawn. It also allows, for example, a child to write and draw a memory that she has never shared and to stick it to the wallpaper in a sealed envelope.

Importantly, too, wallpaper work is fun: it is full of colour and images. It allows the child and the worker to be inventive and imaginative. They get down, literally, on their hands and knees to do it.

Some children may hesitate and say that they cannot write, draw or colour. They should be encouraged to do so – very few people cannot draw or colour – by, for example, getting them to respond to a mistake which the life story worker deliberately makes to bring them into the process because then they will want to correct it. 'No', they will say. 'It wasn't like that, it was like this.'

Life is a journey, and wallpaper allows it to be marked, as one would expect, by dates and events. But wallpaper also allows drawings to be made that are symbolic of journeys along the bottom of the wallpaper. Children choose these themselves – from butterflies and horses to racetracks and bouncing balls, rivers and canals to aeroplanes. One boy asked for a mountain range as his frieze, symbolizing obstacles he had overcome. A girl painted her feet, and her footprints decorated the bottom of her wallpaper. But it is important that the frieze of the child's journey is only pictured from the beginning of her life and not that of the parents or grandparents.

As each ball bounces or each butterfly is drawn, a number should be drawn on the object to identify the year at which the child chronologically is at. Labelling years in this way will help the reader of the wallpaper to reference the age of the child and occurrences recorded by them. A good example of this process is by using a football team such as Liverpool. At one year of age the child has a picture of a goalkeeper, at two, a picture of a right-back defender, and so on. By looking at the unravelled wallpaper, the child and worker can identify how old she was when a picture of a house move is represented on the wallpaper.

Symbols are very important in the work, and children should be encouraged to adopt key codes to express their feelings visually. For example, smiley or sad faces can be attached to experiences or show how children feel about people (see Figure 6.1). One girl insisted on having a spider hanging from a single thread of web on the side of each page of her life story book to show that despite the positive things represented on the page, spiders represented the sadness she felt that she would always have with her.

Confusion was shown by another child by having a rainbow with both sun and cloud behind it. A dark cloud with lots of lightning may express anger. The choice of colours, too – red for anger or blue for confusion – may express how children feel about people and what has happened in their lives.

Figure 6.1 Feelings

Wallpaper is also difficult to destroy. It allows a child to go back and stick new perceptions over events. It allows the child, literally, to walk through her life from the beginning to the age she is now and to see, for example, at what point people intervened and when events occurred, and how one can be related to another even if they are separated by other events.

But wallpaper is not just about events. It is also an opportunity for the child to record memories of those events or record how she reflected on them then, and how she reflects on them now. It allows her to understand how others may have felt at the time. For example, she might come to reflect: 'My mum must have felt sad when dad hit her.'

Making comparisons

Some children draw life-sized shapes of themselves as babies on their wallpaper inside of a life-sized outline of how big they are now. This can have a number of uses to aid their understanding about themselves; for example, what has happened to them as they grew from one size to another. One important thing is that they have survived, whatever has happened to them, which is a positive thing for them to understand. Some workers may wish to fill in the space between the size of the child as a baby and their current size with words or illustrations depicting the positive things that have happened to them during that time of growth.

Comparing sizes can also show how children have grown physically and emphasize their own smallness against the size of adults. For example, a child who was premature (as many of these children often are) can be brought to understand that she was poorly and how she came through that. The shapes children draw of themselves can also show that they are special, a unique person, with their own experience good and bad.

In understanding how big they were as babies or as they grew up, children can be encouraged to think in terms of weight. A worker could go with them to the local supermarket and help them to weigh out their birth weight in produce – like the girl who found that she had equalled two pounds of sugar and a lemon! Or goods can be taken from the kitchen cupboard for the same purpose. The end result is the same as with shapes: children appreciate smallness and vulnerability, but also how they have grown and developed.

Another way of showing a child the different perspectives of adult and child is to reverse roles: the worker gets down to the height of a five-year-old and the five-year-old stands above her on a chair. There can also be role-playing by asking children to put themselves in the place of others and ask for their reactions to events. A child's drawings and other work done in her own time outside of the wallpaper periods can be added to the wallpaper. However, any issues raised during internalization should be resolved within that process and not within the other services, such as therapy or therapeutic parenting. This is not to limit the opportunities for children to explore their feelings in these disciplines, which should happen, but rather to ensure continuity within the life story process.

A journey

Wallpaper work can be completed by a journey – by going back to places significant in the child's life which have featured in the work: the place where she was born and lived; a specially remembered foster home; an event significant in the life of a parent which has impacted on the child's life. While observing what we have said about safety (see Chapter 5), this may be an opportunity to meet those whom children have known in the past, like former carers. Such a journey allows the child to reaffirm where she has come from and where she is going – which is not back to that past. The journey thus allows a child to move on. It also allows things to be changed on the wallpaper as desired as the journey leads her to reassess previously held beliefs about her life; it is often the case that children will do this.

Fun and games

Life story work must have an element of fun – children need to look forward to doing it and to engage with the process. Each session lasts an hour and takes place once a fortnight. It should begin with an informal five minutes of chitchat – How are you? What did we do last time we met? Or maybe a comment on what she is wearing or how nice she looks. There can also be time for a game before the session starts; something disinterested, with no ulterior purpose. This is purely a break – the child's 'tea break'. But it does allow children space to deal with what may be the traumatic events in their lives which they are about to return to. It may also be helpful in managing the child's short attention span with what is being dealt with. It is a time to stop and relax. But children can be so intensely involved in the discussion that they do not want to stop to play. Some children will say that they do not want to talk but want to play. Nothing should be forced; everything should be taken at the child's own pace.

As well as playing as described above, there should also be game playing near the beginning of the session to discover what children understand about their feelings. Charades can be used as they can express anger or sadness and so on, and written cards can also be part of this. Board and other games should offer quick results and be colourful. Such games include Connect 4, Jenga, Snap and Uno. The worker can lose deliberately, but not too obviously, in order to gain reactions from the child – is the child happy or angry about what's happened and how does that compare with what has happened to her at home and in life? If happier or angrier, she can be asked how much more does she feel like that and why.

Games can also be played during the life story process itself, but here the point is not to find out about the child's feelings but to obtain information. For example, Jenga is also available with coloured blocks, which can be used to represent different types of questions. Thus red blocks could represent questions about the child's father, while yellow could be what the child remembers about her mother, and so on. It is important that the worker takes part in this and says what he remembers about, say, his mother. However, it is interesting when children choose to lose or, in the case of games like Jenga, where colours have to be taken, they choose not to take one or to allow the blocks to fall. In some cases, the life story worker will take the opportunity to discuss issues of risk with a child, by using Jenga and the positioning of the bricks within the tower. They will consider how much risk the child may choose to take, how risk is measured and whether she chooses to act on it. This can illustrate whether the child is guarded or reckless in her approach, understanding and concepts of risks.

Other games need no equipment as they can be along the lines of 'One thing I wish I had told my mum' or 'Five things I wish my mum and dad had done to make me safe'.

Games can help children understand their own emotions, for example, a simple card game using cards that illustrate feelings of anger, happiness, sadness, excitement and so on. When the card is turned over to show a feeling, the child – or the worker – can be asked what she or he understands by that word and what they historically or currently associate with it.

Valuing children

Consistency is important in life story work: meetings should be planned and prepared for, they should take place when agreed and the worker should be punctual. This is not only because consistency is important for these children but also because consistency signifies the importance of the work.

It is important, too, that what children feel, say and think should be valued. They must understand that they are respected by how the worker reacts. This means that it is important that they are listened to, not inappropriately interrupted and not contradicted. Because internalization is about dealing with feelings and the child's inner life, children should be allowed to present what they wish to present, to express what they wish to express. It is not necessary to agree with all they say, or with how they think or feel (and a worker may know that something which a child has said is not correct), but it is essential that what is said or felt is respected.

Life story work should never take place until the child has been living in her home for at least three months, but this may be longer, depending on individual circumstances. However, information gathering can begin during those first three months, or even before the child has come into care of the agency. Before sessions themselves begin, it is necessary to agree with a child what she wants to do. At this time, too, as well as meeting with the child, meetings should also be held with the adult who is particularly responsible for the direct care of the child.

Unhelpful kinds of life story work

Prior to the sessions, too, children fill in two books, which cover matters about who they are, their family, who has cared for them and what they think of where they live. It may well be that some children have done some life story work with past workers, though this will not have the detail, intensity or be the kind of approach with which we are concerned here. This work, though, can provide useful reference for the work that needs to be done.

Unfortunately, most of these books would be only factually based; in some cases they may even be inaccurate: for example, with wrong names attributed to photographs. Remarkably enough, the child may have had no involvement and may not even have been shown the book!

Burnell and Archer (2003) make criticisms of some of the life story work they have come across in therapy with adopted children, which 'is often…effected very superficially. Frequently, there is insufficient detail; the truth about the child's traumatic past tends to be glossed over and adopters are not routinely involved' (p.75). Price (2003) says that she has found that some social workers have constructed 'formulaic' life story narratives, which make for 'over-positive interpretations of the child's life experiences' (p.45). She says that Treacher (2000) questioned the therapeutic value of the process and that he suggests 'that its primary function may be in helping practitioners to deal with the implications, for their profession, raised in approaching a child's "unspeakable" distress' (p.47). Fahlberg (1994) refers to the dangers of what lies behind this when she says:

The very fact that adults hesitate to share information about the past with a child implies to him that his past is so bad that he won't be able to cope with it. Whatever the past was the child lived through it and survived, and so can live with the truth. The truth can be presented in a harmful way that lowers the child's self-esteem or in a way that helps the child to understand and accept his past and thus raises his self-esteem.

Another kind of shortcoming is that criticized by Vaughan (2003), who says:

> In our experience many such [life story] books tend to simplify and sanitise the child's past, leaving him with an incoherent and inauthentic story line. An extreme example of this was provided in the life story book of a child who had been sexually abused by her biological father. It contained a photograph of him, bearing the text: 'This is the Dad who loved you'. The child slept with this under her bed. The message this gave the child perpetuated and compounded her confusion between a loving parental relationship and an inappropriate sexual one. (p.160)

It is worth noting all such shortcomings, but also worth remembering that despite them there will still be something of value in the process in what has gone before.

Some thoughts on process

There are children, of course, who have a horror of returning to their past. They should be told that the work will help them make sense of their problems. They may be more likely to be persuaded to embark on it if they see that other children are involved in their own life stories. But if a child refuses to take part and it is thought that she cannot be encouraged to do so, information gathering can still be carried out and the life story written up, if imperfectly.

A contract is another prerequisite of the work. Contracts give purpose to the process, make what is going to happen official and important (thus impressing the child with its seriousness), and make it credible to the child. A contract should involve the child, the key carer and the life story worker. It should clearly state the purpose of the sessions, the rules about sessions (that they are confidential, that expressing feelings during sessions is acceptable, and so on), the times of sessions and their content, and that any questions which the child or the worker wants to ask will be listened to.

Sessions should be part of an integrated process within an agency, which involves the child, the carer, life story worker and therapist. Recognition of this underlines the importance of communication. It also enables everyone working with the child, as well as the child herself, to know what is going on and how each person and each part of the case fits together.

The process is also about confidentiality. There are different groups or rings (see Figure 6.2) comprising the life story worker, the child, the therapist and the therapeutic parent who sit in a ring of confidentiality. The child knows that each talks to the other. This sharing of information helps the child in her relationship with the outside world. There are also other rings of confidentiality: for example, the school, the foster parent and the social worker. However, here sharing is not always observed, to the child's detriment. For example, a foster carer's arm was broken by one child but this wasn't told to the school, because the foster carer

Figure 6.2 Ring of confidentiality

believed that whatever the problems faced in the foster home, the child was doing well at school. Meanwhile the school faced problems with the child but never told the foster carer in the belief that all was well in the foster home. A child in one foster home killed a family pet, but this was never told to the school, where, unknown to the foster carer, the child was tying up other children. Life story work requires the sharing of all information with professionals and those involved in the life story process, such as foster carers. Thus, there should be regular meetings for discussion about each child.

Sessions should be planned seven days in advance and session planning adds clarity to what is being done. What happens at sessions should also be recorded: how the child fared; problems; what was achieved; immediate future action which needs to be taken with the child; and matters which have arisen which may lead the child to other services.

Careful consideration should be given to where sessions will take place – not only the place itself and where it is situated, but also what it looks like: is it comfortable, bright and welcoming, and will it make the child feel at ease? It should be a room which is also private so that there will not be interruptions, and one which is familiar but neutral. There should also be childish objects around – posters and pictures, games and toys. A bedroom may not be a good idea because of what a child may associate with bedrooms. However even where the child regards the bedroom as a safe and special place, the nature of the information shared there may spoil this feeling for her.

Thought should also be given to the time when sessions will take place, remembering, of course, that they have to vie with the other parts of a child's day – mealtimes, school, therapy and the child's leisure time. Before bedtime may seem an obvious time but it should then be asked what could result from the sessions – the memories and feelings – which a child is then left with as she prepares to go to sleep. This means that there should be a significant span of time between the session and when the child goes to bed, if the session is to be held later in the day. Ideally, that time might be when lots of activities are going on – cinema visits or the cub or guide group, homework or watching television. The important thing is that the child goes from a time of memories (the session) to a time of activities, which is followed by bedtime.

Preparation is the key for life story work. The three constituents of this are:

- an understanding of the process
- agreement with the child and other workers about what the process is about
- the choice of the right environment.

If these are not settled, then the work with children can become unstable and unproductive.

The dos and don'ts of beginning

Having laid great emphasis on preparation, it may seem strange to say that there may be problems in actually starting but this can be so. The stumbling block may be the direct work, because anyone undertaking life story work must be confident in their ability to work with children and be able to communicate with them. If a worker does not have the confidence to do this, then he should not attempt the work. Very often social work students on placements are given life story work to do. This fundamentally misunderstands the importance of the work and the skill required to carry it out. It also implies (wrongly) that the life story work can be done in a very limited of time, given that a whole student placement is only 100 days.

Students can be involved in life story, for example, as collectors of information or note takers, and they can identify individuals who would not normally be interviewed but who could be contacted if it was felt that an interview would be worthwhile or that they could help fill in gaps. Students can also be involved in direct work with children on their family tree or creating the life story book. It would be wrong, though, for a student to begin the life story process and then have no opportunity to finish it. Equally, if gathering information, students may not have the experience to interpret, understand or challenge information given to them. They may misinterpret, assume or miss vital details – or all three. This may lead to inaccurate information and, therefore, cause more confusion for the child.

If a student is given the main role as a life story worker this can mean that the process may be curtailed, when, in fact, starting it and then stopping it when incomplete can be damaging to children. It confirms in children's minds what will often have been their experience – that adults are unreliable and that professionals come and go.

Before the life story actually begins, some discussion should take place about why the child is in care. She should be allowed to give her understanding of why she has come to be where she is – she may blame herself, may think it is because mummy could not look after her properly, or that daddy was a threat to her safety.

Mapping family and other relationships

This preparatory work should be followed by work on the child's family tree and how she fits in among its branches. Here colour coding can be used to express how she feels about her relatives. Often who they are will be a surprise to the child – she may not have known why her brother or sister had a different second name to her, or she may not even be aware of brothers or sisters, or half- or step-siblings. There was one girl who believed that her foster family was, in fact, her birth family. Life story work is partly about how the tree's branches sprout and names are added to them.

In a family tree (sometimes called a genogram), the youngest generation sits at the bottom and the oldest generation at the top. Coulshed and Orme (1998) refer to a general function of the genogram:

> Genograms can become a useful talking point for families who, while they are helping the worker to complete them, begin to uncover their family's unwritten rules, myths, secrets and taboos. This map of family relationships can reveal, too, how patterns might get repeated across generations.

In an ecomap, by contrast, children are in the middle and others radiate around them, thus showing them and their importance to the children. These people may or may not be relatives. While parents and brothers and sisters are the closest names spatially (because relationally) to that of the child on a family tree, the closest person on an ecomap could be a grandparent or a foster carer (see Figure 6.3).

As life story work is about helping to clarify a child's life and experience, the ecomap is one way to illustrate the strength or distance of relationships to a child among those people who have entered her life. It is one way, too, of finding out how children themselves regard others – what, for example, does 'father' or 'grandparents' mean to them; there may well be people who are not biological fathers or grandparents but who are, nevertheless, seen as such by the child.

As ecomaps show, those who are related to the child may be more distant from them than those who are not. Nevertheless, all children come from families, so whatever damage has been done to them within

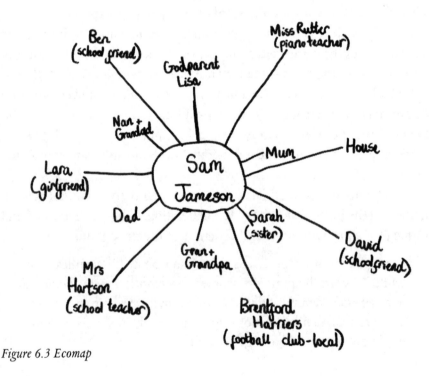

Figure 6.3 Ecomap

that family, consideration must be given in life story work to the child as part of her birth family, to picture her within that family and to chart the relationships with other family members. She may come to know, in the course of the work, that what has happened to, say, her own grandparents in their childhoods may have had an impact decades later on her life. The ecomap performs the same function for people who are not related to the child but who are around the child, showing closeness, distance and relationships.

Viewing family and other relationships in this way may allow children and life story workers to question why, say, a father is placed where he is. There may not be an answer to this, as there may not be answers to other questions which these charts raise (indeed, which the life story process raises); but what is important is that they allow questions to be asked and the answers, although not immediately available, to be provided in time.

The life story worker needs to find out who the child knows in the family and who is related to whom and how. When the child is talking about people, she should be asked to draw them on the wallpaper, using facial expressions, with the child attaching her feelings, by the kind of codes we described on p.95: trust, not trust; like, dislike; distant, close; and so on. The purpose here is not to have the child say that she does not like this person or that person, or prefers this one to that one, but to allow her to demonstrate her feelings. This is a very subtle point to understand. For example, children will often put a smile on a face of a parent, irrespective of what that parent may have done. They may say that the parent was horrible and they may hate them. The picture, however, shows a 'happy' person and could be interpreted as children finding them to be nice, pleasant, kind, and so on. By giving children room for coding feelings with their pictures, the worker is able to consider with the children the importance of the representations.

It may not be difficult for children to say that they hate someone, but it may be very difficult for them to say why they are saying it. They may draw using colours to express anger, or the codes may express anger about, say, their mother, in which case they should be asked why they are indicating anger and how they would explain their feelings towards her. Had they simply been asked to draw their mother without using colours or codes, then they would have had no chance to talk about their feelings towards her. As life story work takes the child through her story, so that she develops a greater understanding of her life and those who have impacted upon it, feelings about people, family members and others may change. Thus, a child's first reaction to a person may well not be the definitive one.

Asking questions, finding answers

Who the child knows in the family is not the same as who is a member of the family, so children should be asked who they know exists – the half-, step- and full brothers and sisters, or others, like parents' other partners. They may well have heard mention of these people but still not know who they are. This can be so for many children in large families where, for example, much older cousins can seem quite separate from a much younger child, or parents' cousins can be transformed into 'aunts' and 'uncles'. How much more confusing can it be, then, for children whose families may not only be large and very complicated but also chaotic.

The chaotic nature of family relationships may be confusing, but even children whose families are more regular may, through being in care, have little idea who they are. One young person told West (1995): 'I was in a history class and we had to draw a family tree and fill it in, and I couldn't do it because I've never seen or know nothing about my natural family.'

An important question that stems from children learning about brothers and sisters of whom they had not been previously aware is 'Where are they?' If they have been adopted, it may not be possible to know, and even if a child wishes to find out, she is not legally entitled to search for them until she is 18 years old.[9] But every effort should still be made by the life story worker, through the adoption team, to find out all he can about other children – that they live in, say, the south east, and that they are happy and healthy. If the child whose story is being written wishes to use a letterbox to convey a message, she should be encouraged to do so, but should also know that there is no guarantee that she will get a reply.

Children can be curious about quite simple but important facts – how old are their grandparents? Are they still alive? They are also curious about very simple facts about themselves – the kind of information which many children pick up casually from their families or parents but which children in care are often denied because of their separation from their family. These are facts like their weight at birth; whether they were born in a hospital or at home; whether their father was present at their birth. There are other, similar questions to be answered – Why were they given their name? Did they have hair at birth and, if so, what colour was it? If their brother or sister was poorly when they were born, were they also poorly? At what age did they say their first words? When did they first walk? Did they walk before their brother and sister did? In particular, asking questions about comparisons is about establishing the fact that they are 'normal', that they are ok, that there is nothing wrong with them. They may have been led to think that there was something wrong when they were unable to be placed for fostering or adoption, or when placements broke down or because they cannot live with their families. There will be many other reasons why this is so, and these reasons they need to know and understand – a very important consideration in internalization.

Another way in which children will sometimes make comparisons is by asking workers about their own birth, growth and childhood. Workers should not shy away from this – after all, they have access to the most intimate details of the child's life, and so life story work should also be seen as being about sharing.

Children's interest in their brothers and sisters, too, is about comparing their respective developmental milestones. Very few of the children engaged in life story work will not have brothers and sisters, or at least half- or stepbrothers and sisters. In those rare cases, such comparisons not being readily available, the worker can discuss how children generally tend to develop. Sometimes, of course, information will have to be given based on what parents have said.

Grace: A child's knowledge

Grace was ten. Before she was born, a man, with whom her mother was having a relationship, slit his throat in front of her mother and two of Grace's older half-sisters, who were then aged 14 and 15. He had preceded his attempted suicide with a threat to murder the three of them. Grace asked about the relationship. The life story worker knew the whole story but did not know how much Grace knew. Thus, it was important to discuss her know-ledge rather than inform her. She had a safe version, which was that a man who had hurt himself and her sisters had 'to go away'.

But what did 'hurting' himself mean? The story of what she believed had happened was often repeated along with the question. Her story never referred to the incident about his cutting his throat; what she knew was that he had hurt himself and problems had resulted from that.

Through discussion and questioning, Grace came to know that she was referring to a story about a man who had known her mother, who had problems in his head and was sad inside and who had hurt himself. Her mother had worried about this and so had helped him to go somewhere where he could be helped, but he never came back to live with the family. There was no need for Grace to know the exact details of what he had done.

Children will also be interested in the events immediately before their birth. These are likely to concern whether they were wanted and cared for; whether dad hit mum; whether she was hit in the stomach when pregnant; or whether she smoked or drank during that time. If she smoked, did she know the dangers or could she not help smoking? There may be answers we have which will serve no purpose in being passed on. For example, if a father has confessed that he kicked the child's mother deliberately to hurt the child, there would be no good to be had from saying so, but the child could be told that dad was unhappy about becoming a father again.

Putting some of the pieces together

Family stories, even when they are trivial, can be very important in the search for meaning. It is important for the life story worker to find out what stories, if any, children know and whether their awareness of them is correct and whether their understanding is harmful or not harmful to them. Stories may be, as we say, trivial but, equally, they may be tragic, sad or happy. They can all be gathered during the interviewing of those who have been involved with the child. Because there is so much sadness and tragedy in the lives of these children, which, inevitably, can cloud their memories, it is important to seek positive stories that show their strong qualities or those of people who have cared for them. For example, there was the boy who discovered that his grandfather had been a champion boxer, and another whose grandfather had been a mayor. Stories are often associated with important events in family life, like weddings, birthdays and Christmas and other festivals, and even stories about funerals may be funny.

Life story work is about the construction of a family for those who have often never known one or who have one where there are pieces missing or one which has become fragmented. Anecdotes can be a way of making that family seem less fragmented.

However, we should not underestimate the difficulties involved. For example, talking about stepparents or stepbrothers and stepsisters, with their implied part in shifting relationships, is very often not easy for a child to understand. What can help here is the use of a movement chart (see Figure 6.4). This is a series of boxes, linked to each other, which record significant events with dates; for example, mother meets father; mother and father live together or marry; child is born; mother meets another man; mother moves in with other man; child of mother and other man born; and so on. Movement boxes are better than a chronological list (though they are run chronologically) because they show events, their consequences and how events two or three boxes back have their impact on later events. Therefore, children are able to begin to understand the process of sequencing and the concept of cause and effect.

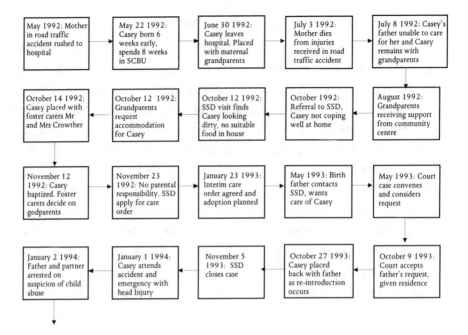

May 1992: Mother in road traffic accident rushed to hospital	May 22 1992: Casey born 6 weeks early, spends 8 weeks in SCBU	June 30 1992: Casey leaves hospital. Placed with maternal grandparents	July 3 1992: Mother dies from injuries received in road traffic accident	July 8 1992: Casey's father unable to care for her and Casey remains with grandparents
October 14 1992: Casey placed with foster carers Mr and Mrs Crowther	October 12 1992: Grandparents request accommodation for Casey	October 12 1992: SSD visit finds Casey looking dirty, no suitable food in house	October 1992: Referral to SSD, Casey not coping well at home	August 1992: Grandparents receiving support from community centre
November 12 1992: Casey baptized. Foster carers decide on godparents	November 23 1992: No parental responsibility. SSD apply for care order	January 23 1993: Interim care order agreed and adoption planned	May 1993: Birth father contacts SSD, wants care of Casey	May 1993: Court case convenes and considers request
January 2 1994: Father and partner arrested on suspicion of child abuse	January 1 1994: Casey attends accident and emergency with head Injury	November 5 1993: SSD closes case	October 27 1993: Casey placed back with father as re-introduction occurs	October 9 1993: Court accepts father's request, given residence

Figure 6.4 Movement chart

The movement chart is a good example of how the confusion of many children, which stems from the chaotic lives of their families, can be dissipated. An example of this concerned Jane. She was helped to make sense of her mother's many moves and with whom she had lived by the use of large, cut-out pictures of houses being set out on the floor for her. Each house had a story, which was explained to her. The names of the people associated with each house and their relationships were written on paper which she then put in the relevant house. Jane was then able to walk around and in and out of each house, so that she could see what had happened to her mother before she was even born. She could see, too, that as people paired off, they moved, taking some other people with them, leaving others behind. But these people were not strangers: they were Jane's full, half- and stepbrothers and stepsisters, cousins, parents, and grandparents.

But such an exercise was about more than acquainting a child like Jane with facts, important though that is. It was also about allowing her to understand and to think about what these moves and relationships mean, and why Jane's mother acted as she did, which may not always have been in her daughter's best interests. Jane, like so many other children in her situation, may well have moved many times, so the exercise also allowed her to connect her mother's itinerant life and her own: she may have reasoned that her mother felt the same way she did. These feelings could be about loss but they could also be about knowing how happy her mother was when she found someone to care for her, just as Jane had been when cared for in her foster home.

The other side of the coin of what children feel about others in their lives is what those people feel about them. If a child is asked what she would ask a family member if she had the chance, she will often say things like 'Do they like me?', 'Do they think of me?', 'Were they pleased when I was born?', 'Was mummy happy when she was pregnant with me?', 'Was she pleased that I was a girl and not a boy?', 'Why did dad do what he did to me?' There will be, of course, questions to which the answer is not known, in which case the worker should say that it is a good question but he does not know the answer. But even if he does know, he has to judge the balance of benefit in telling the child at that stage.

As a rule such information should be shared if a child is able to absorb it and reflect upon it. However, if the child is very young or brittle, and the information might cause hurt, then sharing the information should be discussed with the child's therapist or therapeutic parent. If the answer is positive, then it is important that the answer be given within the life story work and not during therapy. If information is too sensitive to share, the life story worker will record the details separately, and when the child moves on the information is passed to the safekeeping of the new carers. It is hoped that, as the child develops, she will be able to consider the information held and benefit from it.

In much of this questioning, children are seeking affirmation about themselves and of their own value. The temptation here, as elsewhere, is to give them answers, but this should be resisted: it is important that children are encouraged to come to their own answers and understanding, itself a way of developing internalization. Thus, questions should often be reflected back to children – they should be asked what they think the answer might be and why. When questions cease to be asked, it is because children have gained an acceptance of the answers, they have, in fact, internalized that aspect of their lives. When that stage is reached, it is for them to give the answers which they have arrived at in their life story book.

We have discussed what the child needs to know in terms of fact, but around those facts are stories. For example, if father was present at the birth, there may be a story of something he did which was helpful to the child being born, or some amusing story of how he nearly missed being there. Again, there will be the story that emerges from the answer to the question about whether nanny and granddad supported mum when she was pregnant or how they reacted to the news that she was expecting.

Not sharing information will be a rarity, and something which will have been thoroughly discussed between life story worker, therapist and therapeutic parent. But too often information is omitted from life story

Liam: The hot pursuit

Liam was a four-year-old in a large family and his father had three women in his life at the same time: Liam's mother, who was his wife, and two other women. There were ten children in all, and all were taken into care by a large English city local authority. But at one time Liam's father abducted him and another child and took them to Ireland, from where he had come originally.

In Ireland a social worker found Liam with a broken leg resting in a bucket of ice-cold water. Liam was taken to hospital and from there to a foster home. At one time he escaped from the home and he was seen hobbling over the walls of neighbouring gardens pursued by his foster carer, who was also hobbling due to a leg injury. This was a story which mixed elements of sadness and comedy, but also showed Liam's rebelliousness; it was a story of which he had been unaware.

books on the assumption that a child cannot take the information. It is always wrong to assume this. Apart from anything else, the consequence is to lessen the usefulness of the work.

A major question for children is whether they were wanted. This is a very logical question – after all, they do not live with their parents and they are in care. They are asking themselves whether they are in care because they are unwanted or whether there are other reasons why they cannot live with their parents. This can be complicated by the fact that they may know that they have brothers or sisters who still live with their parents. If a child had been taken into care when she was a baby, she could be told that her mother didn't know what she wanted. But if the child had been told many times that she was unwanted, then there is little point in the worker denying it. However, other facts about the child's mother can be given: that, for example, she had mental health problems; that she had too many children to care for; or that she had poor parenting skills.

We have said that a child will often ask very simple questions about herself and her circumstances (as well as very complicated ones). It should, however, also be remembered in doing life story work that a child's world is very simple and an adult's is very complex. Many, many children love their parents even though their parents have acted in terrible ways towards them. It is not always easy to say whether a parent loves a child in the same way. It is true that many parents have done terrible things to children whom they claim to love and, indeed, show every sign of loving them. But even in the 'ordinary' exchange of emotions between a child and a parent, the one does not love the other in the same way, even if they both love each other dearly.

Many parents – and we are not here referring only to parents who are abusive and live chaotic lives – have children with different partners in relationships that are not always compatible: some are better than others; some abusive and some not; some are loving and some not; some of the children were conceived intentionally and some were not. There are parents who have children and move on to a new relationship leaving those children behind (for example, a high proportion of divorced fathers lose contact with their children); they leave behind what they cannot control. Such a complicated emotional world is inconceivable to a child whose first response is 'I love mummy' or 'I love daddy', to offer that unconditional love to which Shakespeare refers: 'Love is not love/ Which alters when it alteration finds' (Sonnet 116). Most parents love their children unconditionally, and children, where they develop healthily, come to understand this instinctively. However, the child who does not experience unconditional love learns as she grows up that there are certain ways in which she has to act in order to receive love, or what she takes to be love, and such ways can be very destructive.

We have discussed what a child wants to know about herself and what she thinks of others and others think of her. The other part of this collection of questions is what the worker thinks of the child's parents. Let us take a child who has been neglected by her mother. It is not for the worker to make moral judgements about a child's mother, but rather for him to explain why the mother may have acted as she did; for example, that she herself had been neglected as a child, that she had never been taught how to look after someone. But that is not to say that what happened was acceptable, and a child should be told that. If a child has been, say, physically abused, we can say that what the parents did was wrong but that things had happened to the child's father when he was a child which left him confused, but, unlike the child, he had had no one to help him deal with what had happened to him.

If workers tell children that a parent is bad, this may lead the child to infer that she is a product of badness and may, thus, be bad herself. Children do not want to hear that they are responsible for what has happened (they are not, but they can conclude that they are). They need to know that while what the parent or parents (or others) did was wrong, there may well be reasons why this happened. In the course of interviewing it can be possible for a parent's apologies to be relayed to the child, along with his or her wish that the child will do well in life.

But while an abuser's own history, abuse or neglect can be made known to the child, along with the fact that he was not lucky enough to receive help, it should be explained to children that everyone has

choices, that we can weigh our actions, and we can consider the consequences of how we act on ourselves and others. Children can be asked
about the hurt which they have felt at the hands of others to indicate
what the consequences can be and, thus, how someone else could feel, or
how they would feel, if they acted in a certain way.

Children can understand that even if they have been abused, abuse is
in the past and they are now being helped to a future where they can
accept their hurt and understand the reasons for it. Then they can live a
happier life that would not be possible without help. It is by understanding what we were that we are able to make safer choices for what we are
to be.

Exercises

1. Keep a reflective account of one day to chart your own
    feelings, recording when you laugh, feel sad, become
    excited, frustrated or confused, and so on.

2. With these feelings in mind, consider how you might
    represent them pictorially or through mime or charades.

3. Are there stories in your life which you have discovered
    were not as told? When you discovered this, how did you
    deal with it?

4. Create your own three-generational family tree where you
    are the middle generation if you or your brothers and sisters
    have children, or the last generation if you and they do not.
    Do not record the individuals by name but consider what it
    is that makes you think of them – for example, an activity, a
    job, a feeling, a memory – and draw these where their
    names would normally appear.

CHAPTER 7

Making the Book

What a life story book is – and is not

In some respects, there is nothing very special about making the life story book, nothing very different from how many authors go about their task. The information has been collected, the interviews have been carried out, and the facts have been checked. The author – the worker – has before him the rough materials: the documents, the wallpaper narrative and such things that have been collected. The task is now to start.

But, of course, in important ways, this is a very different task from the creation of most books, because it is the record of a child's life, often a very unhappy and traumatized one. It will also be the summation of all the work with which the child herself has been engaged in during the previous months, so that she must recognize the outcome as, at very least, being worth all the effort and pain and, at best, helpful to her future progress in life.

Let us be quite clear about what a life story book is. It is not a life story in the accepted, conventional autobiographical sense, although it is an autobiography and it will be roughly chronological; and, of course, it is true that not all autobiographies conform to standard formats of chronological narrative and stating the facts. However, a life story book of the type described here is, first and foremost, a clear account of what happened during the process of internalization. It is where the child has reached at the end of that process; it is much more than a factual account, a series of dates, a chronology. Through it the child needs to recognize what she has done and achieved, what she has come to understand about herself and her life. Even if the book is not always literally true, it is the child's story, where – importantly – misconceptions, which should now find no place between the book's covers, are dissolved.

Writing and the child

The writer is the worker, not the child. We shall refer later in this chapter to the role that children can have in the creation of their books, but the task ahead now is not to go over again what the child knows and believes, or to help her to understand her past – that is part, as we have shown, of amassing the raw materials. Engaging the child as writer or creator would also inordinately lengthen the creation process (which, anyway, will take about 80 hours) to little obvious beneficial effect. However, this does *not* mean that the child is a passive observer in the making of the book. Far from it; as we shall show, there are many ways of involving children – from their choice of themes and illustrations to their approval of the final work. But while children are not, for the most part, the physical creators of the book, its quality will depend on the consistency and quality of the relationship between the child and the life story worker that has gone into the work, and this is part of the creation of the book. That said, it is worth remembering that the life story worker may not be the child's key carer or the most important person in the child's life, who may be, for example, the foster carer.

However, the key carer can have a crucial role in life story work. It is the key carer who is there to support the child after whatever may arise in the session. The key carer can also give the child support if she feels unable to attend the session. That the work of the therapist runs side by side with that of the life story worker, by helping the child deal with what may have been the imparting of very painful information, does not diminish the key carer's role. The key carer, after all, is very much a constant in the child's life – he is *the* special worker, who will see the child most days; will know the child better than most because he will see the child during her ups and downs, during her crises and her good times; knows the dynamics of the family and what is happening at school; and will be part of the child's Looked After Children review. For a child in residential care, the key carer may be the nearest thing she has ever known to a caring parent.

The material

At this stage the information that has been collected will be enormous: movement charts, ecomaps, genograms, statements, photograph albums, newspaper cuttings, official documents, written accounts and tape recordings. These are primary and secondary sources, and some will be directly useful in creating the book, others will be background material to inform what appears.

A major source for the book is, of course, the wallpaper work, and this may be the time to reveal some things the child did not want to discuss or to be known about, which were placed in a sealed envelope. One child had certain bad things that had happened to her placed on flip charts, because she did not want to discuss them and did not want them on her wallpaper. Session plans, too, have information – what were the hopes for the day and the outcomes for the day?

In considering all of this (and more), the worker is, indeed, like the writer of some other kinds of books – he must see how different people's accounts marry up. If they don't, then corroborative evidence for one account or the other must be sought. Such evidence may be, for example, the diaries which foster carers keep, contemporaneous notes made by social workers, court reports, statements made at different times by the child, or second interviews when the worker returned to clarify earlier statements.

But often there may be no corroborative evidence to support one view or another. When this happens all views should be stated and, where possible, the sources named. In such circumstances, the child should be told that people get confused, that memories fade with the passing of time, or that people forget. The child then has the opportunity to decide which statement she wants to believe, or to accept that she has to live with different stories, which is, after all, a not uncommon choice in the lives of many of us.

Creating the book

The making of the book can be done in the worker's office, with all the information spread around and the computer and scanner at the ready. How to make the book is up to each worker. One person may prefer to start with a sketch of what will be on each page. Another may choose to begin creating the book during the internalization process as the child proceeds – almost a live recording, so to speak. In this case, the worker will have put on the computer what had been discussed each day.

And just as each worker can decide for himself how to proceed, so each book must reflect an individual child. There is no template, no right way or wrong way of how the book will turn out or what it will contain.

There is nothing special about the means by which the book is created. All that is needed is a standard computer, with internet access, and a standard scanner and printer. A simple publishing program will be required. PowerPoint is probably best for these purposes as it is more flexible and user-friendly than Word. PowerPoint allows themes, watermarks (which can serve as backdrops to pages over which text and images can be placed) and images to appear in the foreground or background. Another advantage of PowerPoint is that it allows the book to be shown on screen, page by page rather than, as with Word, the user having to scroll down.

Clipart, the artwork which can be used to illustrate the book, can be obtained free and copyright free off the internet (this can be obtained by clicking on 'Insert' and then clicking on 'Picture'). Other images can be found elsewhere on the internet through various search engines, such as Google. However, as printing in colour can be expensive, it may be cheaper to buy stickers or themed paper from a stationery shop to give the book individual touches. The personalisation of the book will lead to the child attaching more value to it. An electronic version of the book – children may prefer a disk of the finished version or both disk and hard copy – allows animation and music.

The worker will need a lot of paper: the average life story book is 150 pages in length. Stationery shops stock a variety of paper, like that with wave or scroll illustrations, suitable for life story books. But these papers should not be used unless the child is taken to a shop and has the chance to choose the paper she wants.

Who tells the story?

Is the book to have a narrator or does the child tell her own story? Ordinarily, the story, written by the worker, has the child telling it in the first person singular. In an audio version children record their stories on tape or they can video their own story. In at least one case, a child spoke the commentary on a video – this is where I was born, this is where I lived, and so on – and so was able to relive his experiences on the spot. But this child was able to regard those places as safe; other children may well not be able to feel that. Each child will have her own memories and have reached her own point in emotional development, so what is done will be at her pace and in her way.

Unlike the child with the video camera, other children will favour different methods and ways of illustration. There is the life story book that is rich in photographs (but this may be thanks to a foster carer who took many); others will rely on clipart off the computer. Because each child is different, so will each book be.

However, there may be children for whom their story remains so painful that they cannot tell it in any of these ways or as a first person written narrative. In such cases it is written in the third person. Some children have had a picture of a favourite teddy bear or a toy dog telling their stories. This removes the responsibility from the child to tell the story herself.

What to show and what to write

If there is a theme it should be discussed with the child: does she want a theme, and if so, what should it be? There can also be a discussion about what picture is to be used on the book's cover. A qualification here is the quality of the preferred picture or illustration and how it ties in with the story being told.

Photographs that can be misconstrued should not be included in the book. These might include pictures of children in a bath or posing suggestively. There may be other photographs, perfectly unexceptionable in other circumstances, which may cause a child grief or distress, so these, too, should not be used. Some pictures, maybe even ones the child has drawn, that were useful for the wallpaper work, may not be a good idea to use in the book. This could be, for example, a picture the child drew showing her father's genitalia or a photograph of the child where she may have scrawled across her face. In this context they may cause hurt, concern or distress. And remember, too, that the book is something that the child may want to show other people, which is a consideration to bear in mind when choosing what to include.

When the book is written, the child can then be asked for her opinion and she can decide if she likes a certain illustration or picture.

What should the book contain? There may be references to things the child owns like a favourite teddy or toy, her most recent school photograph. There may also be reference points like the photograph of a significant place or area. With regard to individuals, it will depend on who they are as to whether or not there is a photograph. For example, it may be distressing for a child to see a photograph of her father, or a child may be returning to an area where the father is known to frequent and be tempted to try to find him. In such cases a drawing – maybe one the child herself made – will suffice (see Figure 7.1). Pictures are, of course, important to all children and will be in the life story book, but it is important that pictures should not overwhelm the words: the printed word must have primacy. The intention is not to have what is no more than a highly elaborate photograph album – this is a story where pictures illustrate what is written, not one where words explain pictures.

Figure 7.1 Mum and Dad

We stated earlier in this chapter that misconceptions should have no place in the book, because they will have been dispelled during internationalization. But there are matters that should actively not be included, for example, any information that has not been discussed with the children in life story (and this may include information they have discussed with their therapist or therapeutic parent). There is a relationship between workers but it is not for the life story worker to put in the book anything that colleagues have told him which has not been part of life story work with the child. If an adult shies away from discussing certain things (although this raises questions about the suitability of the worker and how that person conceives of life story work), then that should not be in the book. Thus, when the child reads the book, there should be no surprises.

Nor is it for the worker to offer his opinions about people, events or the child's reactions to them. The worker should not state in the book, for example, who was right and who was wrong in how the child's parents acted; whether the social services department was lax in protecting the child; or whether a court decision was faulty. Similarly, it is not for the worker to say what he thought happened, to offer interpretation, or offer a view of the child's life. It cannot be emphasized too many times that this is the child's own story and the work is to help the child, who is party to creating the book, whose book it is. But what there *will* be are the comments of others about such matters and descriptions of what happened. However, the final result on the page is what has been recorded about the child's understanding of her life, according to her own knowledge, perceptions and insights. As Fahlberg (1994) reminds us: 'A major aspect of direct work is listening for the child's perceptions. Until we do this, we won't know if we are to expand their information or correct their misconceptions'.

The book should not romanticize, it should not make matters look better than they were. For example, if a child had five placements in as many weeks, she may have believed that this meant that she wasn't wanted. What should be stated is that the moves happened because for various reasons (which are stated) no one could look after the child. Nor, in explaining such a story, should the child's successful placements be idealized.

So, this is a book about a child's story and must emphatically remain so. There should be no diversions into the lives of others or attempts to explain why they acted as they did, although they will have impacted on the child's life. For example a girl may have come to understand during internalization the reason why her father sexually abused her. If her father had been sexually abused as a child, his relationship with his abuser has no place in the book. What the book is recording is simply that this is what happened to him.

Expletives should not be used in life story books, or words like 'paedophile' (an alternative is to say that the person 'did sex things to children' or that he 'liked to hurt children'). Some children use the word that they were 'sexed' by someone. This should not be used because of its vagueness, unless the children show that they fully understand what is meant by the term.

There are matters which can be left out of the book, although they helped the child during internalization. These may include, for example, very graphic details of incidents, to which there will, nevertheless, be some reference, if not an explicit one. But a traumatic incident can be represented by a sad face with tears.

The writing of the book, as has been stated, recognizes the child's emotional, social and intellectual age. With a young child there will be more colour, more pictures (but not forgetting the importance we stated about illustrations always serving the text and not vice versa) and a large type size. Use may be also made of a font suitable for younger children, like Comic Sans or Kids. With younger children, too, the worker may want to include coloured type to emphasize sad, difficult or happy events or emotions.

Younger children tend to compartmentalize events, and the book may need to be created in this way so it accords with how they read it emotionally. Some children will make use of illustrations, for example, because they see their own anger represented in an angry cat (see Figure 7.2), whereas others will see such an illustration for what it is – an angry cat.

Figure 7.2 Angry Cat

Maturity in children means not only their age but also their social and emotional understanding. However, on the matter of age, life story work has been undertaken by children as young as four and as old as 17. Often more mature children seek a more comprehensive, flowing, non-compartmentalized account of their story.

Quotations from the child on the wallpaper should be transposed verbatim to the book because they will show the level of reflection the child was able to attain. The worker should not offer a summary of what a child said, which is likely to be inappropriate to the child's level of maturity. For example, an older child might say: 'I remember when dad was drunk and he used to smack me across the face and it made me feel sad.' This child will have talked about what led up to such incidents, what happened afterward, and what the experience may have been like for the father; and, in some cases, may have been able to reflect on occasions when she had hurt someone and how it felt for her. So the words spoken (and recorded) come from memories and reflection. The younger child simply says: 'My dad used to slap me around the face.' The younger child had not been asked to put herself in another's shoes or to try to remember what she probably could not remember anyway. Thus, what younger children say is much simpler: they repeat what happened factually and may not have the intellectual capacity to reflect on actions.

The role of the child

We said at the beginning of the chapter that the book's author is the worker. We have also shown that children can play a role in the creation of their books, rather than be passive observers. However, some older children can write their own books, although SACCS' experience is that only a few have accomplished this. This came as a result of them saying that they wanted to be involved in the creation of the book. Other children may say this, but that does not mean that they have the capacity to actually write it or, for the reasons already stated, that they should do so. However, if they do express such a wish the opportunity and time it will take should be discussed with them.

There are children who want to have no involvement because their defensive systems or resilience or both prevents them from considering past events of trauma. An active role for a child can be productive, but there should be a firm agreement about how this will work. Importantly, this must involve an understanding by the child that if she fails to turn up at the prearranged sessions, the worker will continue with the task.

The child who wants nothing to do with the creation of the book should be given the opportunity to comment at the end, and what she says, if she objects to any part, should be discussed with her. For any child who objects to anything, there are ways of compromising without jettisoning the integrity and usefulness of the book. If a child objects to a picture, there is usually no reason why it should not be removed. However, should she object to all mention of traumatic incidents these should not be removed but rewritten so that less emphasis is placed on them. Books should be loose-leaf to allow children to remove pages that they do not want others to see. To an extent, this is theoretical because, as we have said, what is in the book is what has been discussed with the child and so should not surprise her.

The usefulness of the book

Life story work looks back. It is about the past and coming to terms with it. But the life story book can also be seen as a passport to the future. The process which the child has gone through for the book to be created lessens the chance of placement breakdown because it gives the potential carer a clear account of what has happened to the child and what to expect from her, as well as explaining behavioural traits. The child, for her part, can see that she is accepted for what she is, lessening her worries that she may be rejected when any new carers find out about her past. The child is not burdened with the guilt of believing that placement breakdown is her fault or that she is unloved.

In some ways, life story books are like a manual about children: this is what they have been through, what they understand about themselves and their experiences and those with whom they interacted, and, crucially, who they are now.

The life story book also gives a voice to the child, something that is so often lacking in childcare, when, in fact, it should accompany placement plans and social workers' reports.

For children themselves, the books are for them to keep, a personal account of their life at the time of writing. It can often have a practical use. We have told elsewhere of what happened with the young woman who wanted to let her boyfriend's parents know who she was. There was also a boy who had visited a consultant for bowel difficulties resulting from his abuse as a baby. He gave the book to his consultant so that he did not have the need to explain all the painful things which had happened to him.

Children in care are constantly having to tell social workers and foster carers their stories, so great is the rate of staff turnover or due to the number of placements that they undergo. As one young person told researchers: 'People keep on coming and going. When you're in the care system that's just what life is'; while another said: 'My social worker seemed to want to find me the perfect placement, so I kept on moving and moving – all over the country' (Blueprint Project 2004).

These are some of the practical uses of the book but it is far more than about matching for placement, giving a voice to children, or children being able to have their stories told without them having to face the ordeal of telling them themselves, important as these things are. It is also about removing the chains which held the child to the past. Fahlberg (1994) asks how a child can move on if she does not know where she has come from. Life story work shows how that journey can be charted, and the book is the story of the journey as the child takes her next and, we hope, safer steps in life.

Exercises

1. Choose a 24-hour period and create a movement chart to account for your day. (The chart should not be more than 20 boxes.)

2. Attach feelings to each box of your movement chart – for example, if you are tired when you get up, you may wish to draw something to illustrate tiredness like a yawn.

3. On a computer using PowerPoint or Word (or if you do not have a computer use several sheets of A4), write the story of your day using the words and pictures illustrating the day in the movement boxes. Then add your feelings using the drawings you have identified in question 2.

4. Consider the finished article and then show it to a colleague or partner and ask him to translate your day, begin a discussion and identify changes to the story as you see appropriate.

CHAPTER 8

But Does It Really Work Like This?

There are children who will have achieved much through therapy and the care they have received. They appear to be happy and they are certainly surviving, so the obvious question is: Why offer them life story work?

As we have stressed, the past is something that must be faced. It does not go away, it cannot be avoided. It may not be ever-present, but it will sometimes be present, perhaps when least expected. At some point this apparently happy, surviving child will ask questions about her past and have thoughts provoked by these questions, or she will be asked questions. These questions or thoughts may arise when there is no therapy readily available because the child is now the adult and away from the care system, or still in the care system but in a situation where, it is believed, she has moved on so therapy is not necessary.

The child who is stuck and other problems

A question to ask about life story work is: Does it really work like this? The word 'process' suggests a continuum, a moving from one stage to the next, maybe with the implication, albeit a false one, that there are no pitfalls along the way. We have described the stages in the process in this book, and from what we have said no reader should believe that there are no stops and diversions and difficulties. But, for most children, the answer to that question about whether it works like this is: 'Yes, it is like this. Life story work can have successful outcomes, despite the problems, if it is done properly.' Some of the things to be done properly will rely wholly on life story workers: how they gather information; how they approach and talk to people they need to interview; their diligence in the work; the wiles and skills they may have to employ to overcome barriers, official and otherwise; most of all, their own suitability for the job and the qualities and skills they bring to it, which influences their relationship with the child.

Life story work, though, it must be remembered, is a co-operative venture, and the most important partner for a life story worker is the child. Children who have suffered horrendous abuse, who may be deeply disturbed, who are confused and distrustful – such children need great professional skills and exceptional personal qualities to be worked with.

There is no such thing as an 'ordinary' or 'average' child when it comes to life story work, just as no child is 'average' or 'ordinary'. Children who engage in this work successfully all do so with support, some needing it much more than others. But what of the child who is stuck, the child who cannot move forward?

Fahlberg (no date) says of children who have been abused who become stuck: 'They may psychologically defend themselves either by withdrawing or avoiding adult–child interactions, or by asserting themselves so that they control the relationship and what happens to them' (p.3). Fahlberg is referring here to children in placement, but much of what she says applies to children who get stuck in life story work, particularly the reference to withdrawal from or avoiding relationships with adults.

But even one child who is stuck is different from the next child, and while there are children who are stuck, there will be others who only appear to be. The reality is that there are some children who do not want to go back to their past. They accept what has happened, they attempt to continue with their lives and they accept that that's it – they cannot take the risk of looking back.

Becky: Assuming the guilt

Becky, 11, was working well on her life story on issues like her carers, why she was in care, what she thought of herself and her life. The problem arose when she came to consider her family. She had had no contact with her mother, who remained an unknown quantity, for two years; it was thought that she might want to remove her daughter from care or cause other kinds of problems. The local authority was hesitant about her mother being interviewed for the work but there was little in the way of information in the social services' files about Becky's family or her history.

A year after Becky had been placed, the local authority relented and the life story worker met her mother and her mother's current partner. She gave information about the child's past, including photographs of Becky when she lived with her parents. It turned out that Becky's grandfather was a senior manager in his profession who because of his job had lived in Zimbabwe. It was a good life, with servants, but he had abused Becky's mother until she was in her 20s.

When her mother needed money, her father said that he would give it to her if she went to Africa. Becky and her baby brother had gone with her. While there the baby had become ill. Becky's mother had inadvertently given the baby too strong a dose of his medicine. Becky found the baby dead in his cot, and came down and told her mother and grandfather that the baby had died. Her mother dismissed her. 'Don't be so nasty – go away!' Although there was a coroner's inquiry in England on their return, Becky had never mentioned her brother again.

In Becky's family tree there was no brother and no father. The family tree could now be completed and Becky was able to talk about the matter factually. She was able to write her mother's story but not her own; to this she could only listen. She talked about her brother – how old would he be now? What did her mother think of her? Did her mother wish that her brother had lived and not Becky? If her brother were alive, would he be living with her?

Her view, which emerged, was that she had thought herself responsible for her brother's death and that was why she was in care. This illusion would not have been dispelled by her being told by the life story worker that she was not responsible; only her mother telling her, through the interview, could remove the guilt that she felt.

Then there are children, similar to those mentioned above, who, effectively, say that they know what happened to them (and they do); that their parents did not protect them; and they want to get on with their lives. At this stage, they have a valid reason not to engage in the work.

Other children take part in the process as a means of encouraging exploration, and because it affords an opportunity for them to ask questions. But when those questions evoke painful answers, they may conclude that it is safer to go no further, to seek comfort in the unknown.

Another group of children who resist are those who are not distressed when doing life story but are affected by the world outside it. They are also aggressive to those outside of the work. Such behaviour may be a sign that they feel unsafe, which means that one of the prerequisites for the work is not being met.

What then is to be done, if it is true, as we say, that, unresolved, the past will some day come back to haunt one? The first thing to say is that children should never be forced into life story work. It is no good telling them that it will be for their own good and stating all the advantages. Children do not reason like that (do adults?). What they see, in all kinds of circumstances – the first day at school, going to the dentist's, eating the nasty-tasting main course – is the main obstacle, not the positive outcome (new friends, healthy teeth, ice cream for dessert). A child who resists life story work should not be forced or induced to undertake it at the beginning of the placement.

Children can become stuck in other ways. For example, they may have no difficulty in identifying factual accounts of what happened to them but be unable to take in what such events mean mentally or emotionally (see, for example, Anne's story, Chapter 2). It is rather like doing mathematical calculations by using a computer but without any concept of numbers. For a worker to avoid causing pain to the child or to himself, is to acquiesce in the child being stuck.

In many of these cases, life story work should continue to be mentioned and opportunities sought to engage the child. For example, a child may resist being the subject of the work in order to avoid the pain it can bring. In which case, stories can be told and recorded in the third person, as we have said. Remember, too, that life story work can be fun and positive, and this aspect of it can be used to encourage children's participation. There are, it is true, many painful encounters for children, much unhappiness to recall, and many frightening memories to face. But there are also happy times to be remembered, loving and helpful people to recall, school and other achievements to be recorded.

As we have shown, life story work has three parts: information gathering, internalization, and the creation of the book. All children at SACCS will take part in the information part if they cannot engage in internalization. If the child persists in resisting, then the book will emerge as a third person narrative, as we have explained in Chapter 7; it can then be given to new carers ready for the time when the child feels able to discuss it and ask questions about the past.

With some children, life story workers will have to weigh up the benefits of persisting in trying to engage them. This may show that there are some children for whom life story work cannot be carried out. This is, however, a small minority, and in the experience of SACCS only three children in seven years have been like this. Sometimes, it is not that children cannot be persuaded, it is that the worker does not have the skills to make this happen.

There may be very simple and easily remedied reasons why a child seems to be stuck. For example, she does not gel with (or even like) the worker; or the environment in which the work takes place does not suit (for example, it is too noisy or too quiet). Then there may be other things happening in the child's life which make life story work more difficult than it would otherwise be (for example, the child is going through a bad time in therapy or has had contact with someone from the past who

Natalie: Choosing who mucks out the horses

Natalie had been labelled as a manipulative nine-year-old whose foster placement had broken down due to her sexualized behaviour and problems of attachment. One of three children, she had been taken into care after being neglected and emotionally deprived by a mother who entered a relationship with a sex offender.

However, when in residential care she was fully engaged in the house where she lived, did well at school and had a good rapport with adults. Her more destructive behaviour had lessened. She took to life story work but could not talk about her abuse; indeed, she would say that she did not *want* to talk about it. But while she was able to talk about her mother's inability to protect her, she could not talk about who had been involved in her mistreatment.

Natalie's mother was interviewed and was reasonably open about some of the people in her life and what Natalie had suffered. It was not regarded as helpful to tell Natalie the names of these people, because life story work is about exploration and children's own memories, not about being told what happened.

Natalie liked horses and went riding. When she did her wallpaper work, her life story worker drew a racetrack. Hurdles were drawn to represent her birthdays. She drew a picture of herself sitting on a horse and also a picture of a cup as a prize for a race. She was asked whom she would like to race against and she named and drew friends and a couple of the adults who worked with her. It was suggested to her that to be a fair race, she would need to draw judges, who would be people she could trust and who did their best by her. She drew her home manager, the life story worker, her mother, which surprised the life story worker, and her social worker. When she drew those who would watch the race and celebrate her victory, they were people in her home – adults and children – and others from school, her riding school and people from the past whom she liked, like her brother and sister.

The life story worker drew a stable block for the horses, and Natalie was told that that was where they went to the toilet so there needed to be people in the drawing who dealt with that. But she was also told that there were no shovels in the stables but only spoons to clear up the horse muck. Who could work there? 'Mike', she said. In a later session she named other men who would work in the stables mucking out the horses with spoons. Eventually, this allowed Natalie to talk about who these men were and what they had done to her.

evokes disturbing memories). Again, it may be that someone important to the child, like a foster carer or social worker, is leaving her life. Or, it may just be that the life story worker has not planned the sessions properly so that they sit well with other parts of the child's life.

There are times when something as simple and everyday as a discussion with the child may reveal that she is not so much stuck as that she cannot find the words to describe how she feels or what she remembers, or how to ask questions about the events in her life, although she wants to do so.

When there appear to be real problems of being stuck, workers need to think imaginatively. For example, we think of life story telling and narrative as being something which goes forward. But does it need to be? There is no reason why the story should not be told backwards if a child feels safer and able to engage that way. The story is then based on the child's currently secure and safe foundations back to a time of loss and separation, from the child's life to that of their parents and grandparents, rather than the conventional situation of vice versa, then why not? The outcome for the child, after all, is what counts.

Personal qualities

Such a discussion brings us to the question of what workers need to bring to life story work. Work with children is not child's play, and anyone doing such work requires certain professional and personal qualities and skills, all of which the life story worker should possess. Paramount in this work are perseverance, imagination, the ability to engage very fully with children at a very profound level over an appreciable period of time, and a commitment which does not falter in the face of difficulty – either on the part of the child or others. It would have been very easy to have given up in cases like those of Becky and Natalie (see case examples 'Becky: Assuming the guilt' and 'Natalie: Choosing who mucks out the horses'), but their cases demonstrate that imagination and perseverance can bear fruit.

CHAPTER 9

Life After Life Story

In one sense the end of life story work is the production of the life story book. In the creation of that, as we hope that we have shown, children have come to a greater emotional understanding and acceptance of their past, about what happened to them and why, and they will have reached the stage where recovery allows them to look positively towards the future. However, it is a common misconception that working through internalization and completing the book brings life story work to an end. It does not. A child who has reached this stage will be at an age when she is able, if that was not already the case, to move to foster care or adoption. But whether adopted or fostered, these children, like all children, whatever their circumstances, have a life to live.

We have emphasized that life story work is a process, and it is that, rather than the book itself, which is the important thing, but it is also a *continuing* and a *living* process. It is something, therefore, which can be continued by the child's new carers, albeit now for different reasons, as the child has passed through the crucial stage of internalization. This means that the book can continue to be extended, to record the many events and occurrences and people who enter the child's life: the new carers and their family; holidays and outings; new interests and hobbies; moving schools; achievements at school and elsewhere; and new school friends, as well as the loss of some people as school and homes change, just as happens to any child.

The life story book will already have recorded the many bad things which happened in the child's life, as well as what the child has gained and achieved. As a new, healthier and more hopeful period begins to emerge, recording in the book catches the new balance, where, we hope, the positive outweighs the negative. Eventually, looking back, with the aid of the book, the child will be able to see a better balance through her *whole* life.

It is likely that the child, given the stage which she has now reached, will feel able herself to add to the book, but, as with past work, this cannot happen without the commitment, enthusiasm and support of those who are her carers.

The past is never past

One fundamental mistake made by some new carers is to welcome a child to a new and permanent environment by saying that this is where her new life begins and that the past is past. This is saying that a door can be closed, locked and never reopened. That doesn't happen for the children about whom we write, any more than it does for any of us. One of the continuing themes of this book has been to emphasize that the past is always with us. We cannot dismiss, ignore or obliterate it. If we try to do so, it will catch up with us, in one way or another, one day. Rather it is how we deal with our past that is the key to our present and future.

To say to a child coming into more permanent care that the past is now gone is also to diminish the importance of that past. Yet this was a past that the child faced; where she struggled to get through the tangle of misconception, confusion and pain; and summoned up the courage to challenge the demons which will have haunted her. Perhaps, the greatest achievement in the life of any child in such circumstances will prove to be just that – and that is no mean achievement. Life story books do not come with a child to a new home to be placed metaphorically, or even literally, in the attic.

It is, thus, important that new carers should understand this, but also that they should be familiar with the purposes of life story work, as well as helping them to continue it. Foster care offers a new home for children, the kind of loving and warm family that they have hitherto not known. Children going to a foster family will become a part of that family's life, just as that family's life will absorb the child – friends, interests, holidays, relatives; the ups and the downs, the difficulties and the triumphs. Making life story a part of that not only encourages children's continuing recovery but increases a family's self-awareness as carers. It enables children to continue their journey in life and takes them into young adulthood.

Life story work is also one way (and an enjoyable one) in which carers can show their commitment to the child, just as, in a different way, the child will have seen the commitment of the life story worker.

Hartley (1953) begins his novel *The Go-Between* with the words: 'The past is a foreign country: they do things differently there.' We can often look back and wonder if the 'I' who is at the centre of our memories is really 'me', if we really knew the other characters, if the events really happened to 'me'. In a new and loving home, children will learn that, indeed, things are done very differently from the home in which they grew up. Colston, Hartley's protagonist, discovers a diary and other relics which take him back to the events of which he was a part 50 years before. Just as he moves from one 'country' to another, so will the children who feature in this book. Like Colston, they will need a map to help them to continue on their way, but they will also be able to look back and, now, to do so with pride at their achievement in the journey thus far taken. That map is life story work.

Notes

1. See, for example, Gibson, F. (2004) *The Past in the Present: Reminiscence Work in Health and Social Care*, Baltimore, MD: Health Professions Press; and Haight, B. (1998) 'Use of life review/life story books in families with Alzheimer's disease', in P. Schweitzer (ed) *Reminiscence in Dementia Care*, London: Age Exchange.

2. We were not alone in finding it difficult to determine just how many needs Maslow had listed in his hierarchy – five or seven. This is a problem caused by later development of the list by others. We are grateful to Professor Martin Davies, author of an entry on the hierarchy in his own *Blackwell Encyclopaedia of Social Work*, for engaging in some desk research to clear up the confusion. The following explanation (given in a personal communication) is wholly Professor Davies's and we quote it here at some length because we believe that, notwithstanding the reservations about the hierarchy referred to below, Maslow's formulation has something to say about children who have been traumatized through abuse – something which, so far as we are aware, no other writers in this field have remarked upon.

    Davies says that in the 1954 first edition of *Motivation and Personality* (Maslow 1954) Maslow does not use the diagrammatic ladder with which we are now familiar. He describes the five key elements in the hierarchy (sometimes also called the 'hierarchy of motivation'). These are physiological; safety; belongingness and love; esteem; and self-actualization. He calls the first four 'deficiency needs' and the last a collection of 'growth needs'. Having given them capitalized sub-headings of their own, Maslow then goes on to describe two 'needs', of which he says 'we know very little': 'the desire to know and to understand' and aesthetic needs. He says that these are important but he does not include them in the five-step hierarchy. He emphasizes that the hierarchy is not rigid and he predicts some of the criticisms that would be later levelled at it – and the way in which exceptions can be identified. A frequent example is that of the hunger striker (a modern equivalent, says Davies, would be the suicide bomber). Davies continues:

> In other words, it isn't a model of motivation that can conceivably explain all human behaviour and I don't think that Maslow was arguing as much. He is arguing that, under many circumstances, human beings can only be expected to move onto a satisfaction of 'higher-order' needs when their basic needs for survival (food, drink, shelter etc) are met. And he was particularly interested in the subject of self-actualisation and how it presented challenges to those who no longer had to worry about their 'deficiency needs'.

Davies goes on to explain that it was two later authors, Madsen (1964) and Roe (1956), who fitted cognitive and aesthetic needs into the hierarchy between the need for esteem and the need for self-actualization. Another writer, Huizinga (1970), who explicitly acknowledges how Madsen and Roe had added to the list, was able to expand the hierarchy to seven without allowing for cognitive and aesthetic needs. He split two of the needs in two – belongingness and love could be passive (the need to be loved) and active (the need to love, to be kind, to help others); while esteem could be active (the need for self-respect) and passive (the need to be respected by others). This formulation was not widely adopted, 'perhaps fortunately', remarks Davies.

Davies points out that empiricists state that all attempts to prove the theoretical legitimacy of the hierarchy have failed to deliver a 'proof'. He says:

> That does not stop it being a helpful aid to thought, policy or practice, but I see it as a crude macro-model at a time when our understanding of influences upon the minutiae of human relationships and behaviour has become very much more sophisticated than it was 50 years ago when Maslow was doing his scholarship.

As we said, we believe that the hierarchy can be applied to traumatized children. We share Davies's views about the hierarchy's imperfections and, of course, do not state its use dogmatically for our purposes, but we do believe it can shed a useful light on them.

3. See especially Fernando, S. (ed.) (1995) *Mental Health in a Multi-ethnic Society: A Multi-disciplinary Handbook*, London: Routledge; Robinson, L. (1995) *Psychology for Social Workers: Black Perspectives*, London: Routledge; and Root, M. (ed.) (1996) *The Multi-racial Experience*, London: Sage.

4. See also Bowlby, J. (1973) *Separation, Anxiety and Anger*, London: Hogarth Press; Bowlby, J. (1980) *Loss: Sadness and Depression*, London: Hogarth Press; Howe, D. (1995) *Attachment Theory for Social Work Practice*, Basingstoke: Macmillan; and Howe, D., Brandon, M., Hinings, D. and Schofield, G. (1999) *Attachment Theory, Child Maltreatment and Family Support*, Basingstoke: Macmillan.

5. See Holman, B. (1995) *Evacuation: A Very British Revolution*, Oxford: Lion.

6. For a summary of recent research see Glaser, D. (2001) 'Child abuse, neglect and the brain: A review', *Journal of Child Psychology and Psychiatry and Allied Disciplines 41*, 1, 97–116; and Balbernie, R. (2001) 'Circuits and circumstances: The neurobiological consequences of early relationship experiences and how they shape later behaviour', *Journal of Child Psychotherapy 27*, 3, 237–255.

7. Children who have been abused may have a false model of parenting in their minds, where love equals sex, sex equals hurting and so on. The need is to provide the children with another model of parenting, one which tells the child that she is cared for, loved and nurtured, that her needs will be met, and that she will be listened to without having to give in return.

   Therapeutic parenting is not in itself therapy but supports the therapeutic process. It encourages those working with the children to look at the issues beneath a child's presenting behaviour and allow the child to express her pain. It encourages workers to be self-aware and understand what they carry emotionally before they unconsciously offload it onto vulnerable children.

8. Internalization is used here as distinct from its technical meaning in psychoanalysis, which states that a relationship with an instinctual object is absorbed into one's mental apparatus, as when a child's relationship with an authoritarian father is internalized as the relationship between an ego and a strict superego. In Kleinian analysis the term is an alternative for introjection: fantasizing the absorption of the whole object or a part object.

9. For information about adoption, search and reunion see J. Feast and T. Philpot (2003) *Searching Questions. Identity, Origins and Adoption*, London: BAAF Adoption and Fostering.

References

Archer, C. (2003) 'Weft and warp: Developmental impact of trauma and implications for healing.' In C. Archer and A. Burnell (eds) *Trauma, Attachment and Family Permanence: Fear Can Stop You Loving.* London: Jessica Kingsley Publishers.

Blueprint Project (2004) *Start with the Child, Stay with the Child.* London: Voice for the Child in Care/National Children's Bureau.

Bowlby, J. (1969) *Attachment and Loss: Vol.1 Attachment.* London: Hogarth Press.

Burnell, A. with Archer, C. (2003) 'Setting up the loom: Attachment theory revisited.' In C. Archer and A. Burnell (eds) *Trauma, Attachment and Family Permanence: Fear Can Stop You Loving.* London: Jessica Kingsley Publishers.

Connor, T., Sclare, I., Dunbar, D. and Elliffe, J. (1985) 'Making a life story book.' *Adoption and Fostering 9,* 2.

Coopersmith, S. (1967) *The Antecedents of Self-esteem.* San Francisco, CA: W.H. Freeman.

Coulshed, V. and Orme, J. (1998) *Social Work Practice: An Introduction* (3rd edition). Basingstoke: Palgrave.

Curtis, P. and Owen, P. (no date) *Techniques of Working with Children.* Unpublished.

Davies, M. (2000) 'Needs, Maslow's hierarchy.' In M. Davies (ed) *The Blackwell Encyclopaedia of Social Work.* Oxford: Blackwell.

Fahlberg, V.I. (1994) *A Child's Journey Through Placement.* London: BAAF Adoption and Fostering.

Fahlberg, V.I. (no date) *The Child Who Is 'Stuck'.* www.adoption.com

Hartley, L.P. (1953) *The Go-Between.* London: Hamish Hamilton.

Howe, D. (2000) 'Attachment theory.' In M Davies (ed) *The Blackwell Encyclopaedia of Social Work.* Oxford: Blackwell.

Huizinga, G. (1970) *Maslow's Need Hierarchy in the Social Work Situation.* Groningen: Wolters, Noordhoff.

Krog, A. (1998) *Country of My Skull.* Johannesburg: Random House.

Levy, T. and Orlans, M. (1998) *Attachment, Trauma and Healing: Understanding and Treating Attachment Disorder in Children and Families.* Washington, DC: Child Welfare League of America.

Madsen, K.B. (1964) *Theories of Motivation: A Comparative Study of Modern Theories of Motivation.* Cleveland, OH: Howard Allen.

Maslow, A.H. (1954) *Motivation and Personality.* New York: Harper and Row.

Moore, J. (1985) *The ABC of Child Abuse Work.* Aldershot: Gower.

Nicholls, E. (2003) 'Model answer.' *Community Care,* 3–9 July, pp.32–34.

Perry, B. (1999) 'The memories of states: How the brain receives and retrieves traumatic experience.' In J. Goodwin and R. Attias (eds) *Splintered Reflections. Images of the Body in Trauma.* New York: Basic Books.

Price, P. (2003) '"The coherent narrative": Realism, resources and responsibility in family permanence.' In C. Archer and A. Burnell (eds) *Trauma, Attachment and Family Permanence: Fear Can Stop You Loving.* London: Jessica Kingsley Publishers.

Roe, A. (1956) *The Psychology of Occupations.* New York: Wiley.

Ryan, T. and Walker, R. (2003) *Life Story Work: A Practical Guide to Helping Children Understand Their Past.* London: BAAF Adoption and Fostering.

Schore, A. (1994) *After Regulation and the Origin of the Self.* Hillsdale, NJ: Lawrence Erlbaum Associates.

Solomon, J. and George, C. (1999) 'The place of disorganization in attachment theory: Linking classic observations with contemporary findings.' In J. Solomon and C. George (eds) *Attachment Disorganization.* New York: Guilford Press.

Treacher, A. (2000) 'Narrative and fantasy in adoption: Towards a different theoretical understanding.' In A. Treacher and I. Katz (eds) *The Dynamics of Adoption.* London: Jessica Kingsley Publishers.

Vaughan, J. (2003) 'The rationale for the intensive programme.' In C. Archer and A. Burnell (eds) *Trauma, Attachment and Family Placement: Fear Can Stop You Loving.* London: Jessica Kingsley Publishers.

West, A. (1995) *You're on Your Own: Young People's Research on Leaving Care.* London: Save the Children.

YoungMinds (2004) *Mental Health in Infancy.* London: YoungMinds.

The Story of SACCS

Sexual abuse was at one time most commonly referred to as incest and was thought to occur only in isolated pockets. In the 1960s and 1970s it began to emerge as the battered baby syndrome. Until then the early professional agendas had tended to concentrate very much on physical abuse and neglect, but then a series of official inquiries, resulting from scandals, brought it very much to the fore in the minds of professionals, the public and the media.

The challenge in the early 1980s for the social worker in child protection was to deal with this new phenomenon as part of everyday practice. Social workers had to develop new skills to communicate with children on a subject which they, as adults, had difficulty with, that is talking about sex and sexuality, and, moreover, doing this in a way that could withstand the rigours of legal scrutiny.

It was at this point that Mary Walsh, now chief executive of SACCS, got together with a colleague, Madge Bray, who was working to help disturbed children communicate by using toys. Together, they looked at how they could adapt the use of the toy box to help this very vulnerable group of children communicate their distress, especially about the abuse they had suffered. Above all they wanted to give children a voice in decisions that would be made about them, particularly in court.

SACCS comes into being

Working within the culture of uncertainty and confusion that prevailed at the time, Mary Walsh and Madge Bray became disenchanted at the lack of time and resources available to do this work properly. They saw no alternative: in January 1987 they left their secure local authority jobs and took it upon themselves to meet the profound needs of the deeply traumatized children who they were seeing every day and who found themselves effectively lost and without any influence on their futures.

SACCS came into being in Madge Bray's back bedroom – the typewriter had to be unplugged to use the photocopier! Demand for the venture on which they were now embarked soon became apparent: they were inundated with requests to see children and help them to communicate about their distress. Mary Walsh and

Madge Bray worked with children all over the country, helping them to tell their stories, giving comfort and allowing them to express their pain. They also acted as advocate for children in court and other decision-making bodies, and as case consultants to local authorities. Through this process, as expected, they began to notice that many of the children were changing and beginning to find some resolution to their difficulties.

They also became aware that there were some very small children who, because of what had happened to them, were either too eroticized or too disturbed to be placed in foster care. Foster carers who were not prepared or trained to deal with very challenging situations day-to-day would quickly become weighed down by the child's sexualized behaviour, and the placement would break down. The real cause of these breakdowns was never acknowledged and, therefore, never dealt with. In time these children were labelled as unfosterable and placed in residential care along with adolescents on remand.

Leaps and Bounds

The heartbreak of watching this happen to three-, four- and five-year-old children was unacceptable. The need was be able to hold the children and their behaviour lovingly, while they were helped to understand and deal with the root cause of their behaviour. The result was the setting up of Leaps and Bounds, SACCS' first residential care provision.

The birth was a long and difficult one, but after three years the first house, Hopscotch, was opened. It filled up immediately, and the children were cared for by staff trained to understand the issues and encouraged to put that four-letter word, *love*, into everything they did.

Many of the children placed in Leaps and Bounds had experienced many placement breakdowns; some had been placed for adoption that had subsequently failed; most had incoherent life histories; some had lost touch with members of their family; and one child, incredibly, had acquired the wrong name. The great need was to find all of this information that was lost in the system, and so the life story service came into existence, to help to piece together the fabric of the children's lives and give them back their own identity.

In addition, a team of professional play therapists was engaged to work with the children in Hopscotch, and subsequently at the new houses – Somersault, Cartwheel, Handstand, Leapfrog and others – while continuing to bring the special SACCS approach to children who were not in residential care.

Within SACCS all those charged with responsibility for the wellbeing of the child were (and are) expected to share information with each other, so that the child's reality and care is held by the whole team.

Find Us, Keep Us

The expectation at SACCS was that when children had come to terms with what had happened to them and were ready to move on, their local authorities would find foster families for them. This proved not to be the case in many instances, and children who had worked hard to recover and desperately wanted to be part of a family would have their hopes dashed. As a result their behaviour deteriorated, and it was extremely difficult to watch this happening, especially as the next part of the work needed to be done within a family.

Leaps and Bounds was never intended to become a permanent placement for the children, so looking for potential foster families and training them to care for this very challenging and vulnerable group of children became the responsibility of a new part of SACCS – Find Us, Keep Us, the fostering and family placement arm of the organization.

Flying Colours

In 1997 Flying Colours was opened. It was a new project designed to meet the needs of young adolescents. Often these were children who had been traumatized when they were very young, but had only just started to talk about it.

As a therapist, Mary Walsh had worked with many such young people, who were not being held in a safe and contained holding environment. She knew that they often run away when feelings overwhelm them, and sometimes end up living hand to mouth on inner city streets, involved in prostitution, drug taking and worse. Flying Colours offered these young people the same loving and nurturing therapeutic care as the younger children in Leaps and Bounds, while at the same time meeting their different developmental needs.

SACCS Care

In 2003 a major rationalization was undertaken to integrate all of the SACCS services which had evolved since the organization's early days. A new company, SACCS Care, was formed, with an organizational focus on the parenting aspect of therapeutic care. This is arguably the most important job carried out with children, some of whom have similar developmental profiles to the most dangerous adults in our society. SACCS believes that unless this issue is addressed properly, traumatized children cannot have a positive experience of parenting, and when the time comes will be unable to parent their own children appropriately.

Today and tomorrow

SACCS provides an integrated model of therapeutic parenting, play therapy, and life story work and education support individually tailored to meet children's needs, coupled with a family placement service for those who are ready to move into a family environment. The SACCS model is underpinned by a complex structure of practice training and clinical supervision, and these standards of excellence have positioned the organization as a national leader in therapeutic care and recovery.

There are many children outside SACCS struggling with the enormous trauma caused by abuse and neglect, children whose experience has taught them that families are dangerous places in which to live. SACCS believes that every child has a right to the expert therapeutic care which can help them to recover from their emotional injuries, but for these children the specialist services they require are often not available.

The next step in the SACCS story will be the establishment of a charitable trust that will underpin a college, training carers in the unique SACCS model. The wider implications are that this training can ultimately inform practice with traumatized children everywhere.

The Authors

Richard Rose is deputy director (practice development) and responsible for life story work in SACCS. He is also a practice teacher. He began his social work career in 1984 when he was appointed a residential care worker for a children's home in Swindon. He obtained a CQSW and Diploma in Social Studies in 1989 and worked in a child and family team in Swindon. In 1991 he moved to Shropshire to become senior social worker in Shropshire's child protection team, becoming a practice teacher in 1996. In 1997 he left the statutory services and was employed with SACCS as a life story practitioner. In 2002 he was awarded a Post-Qualifying Social Work Child Care Award and a BPhil in childcare. He is currently studying for an MBA.

Terry Philpot is a journalist and writer and is a regular contributor to, among others, *The Tablet* and *Times Higher Education Supplement*. He was formerly editor of *Community Care*. He has written and edited several books, the latest of which are (with Anthony Douglas) *Adoption: Changing Families, Changing Times* (Routledge 2002), (with Julia Feast) *Searching Questions: Identity, Origins and Adoption* (BAAF Adoption and Fostering 2003) and (with Clive Sellick and June Thoburn) *What Works in Foster Care and Adoption?* (Barnardo's 2004). He has also published reports on private fostering, kinship care, and residential care for older people run by the Catholic Church. He is a trustee of Rainer, the Centre for Policy on Ageing, and the Social Care Institute for Excellence. He is an associate of the Children and Families Research Unit, De Montfort University. He has won several awards for journalism.

Subject Index

Author Index